Getting
Unstuck

Getting Unstuck

*A Guide to Discovering
Your Next Career Path*

Timothy Butler

Harvard Business Press
Boston, Massachusetts

Paperback edition ISBN: 978-1-4221-3232-6
Hardcover edition ISBN: 978-1-4221-0225-1

Library of Congress cataloging information forthcoming

To Linda, Kiera, Amelia, and my parents,

to my good friend Jim,

and to all of my teachers.

The way up and the way down are one and the same.

—Heraclitus

CONTENTS

ACKNOWLEDGMENTS

Many people have made this book and the work on which it is based possible. Psychology is itself a form of disciplined storytelling, a reflection on human experience that, in the end, comes to us one unique story at a time. First to thank then are my students and clients from whom I have learned so much. Some of their stories appear in the pages that follow, but each has trusted me to share and participate in his or her unique experience at a time of career or life impasse.

At the Harvard Business School, I have received generous support and encouragement for my work from Steve Nelson, Executive Director of the MBA Program, and from two MBA program faculty chairpersons, Carl Kester and Rick Ruback. These individuals, along with deans Kim Clark and Jay Light, have been generous in their support of the MBA coaching program and of my research efforts. The staff of MBA Career Services have been great colleagues and fellow coaches from whom I have learned much. Their management talent and dedication has allowed my research and writing work to continue amid the busy demands of an office that offers thousands of coaching sessions every year. In particular, I would like to acknowledge Jana Kierstead, Lauren Murphy, Betsy Strickland, Mat Merrick, and Stacey Kessel.

Jim Waldroop and Dave LeLacheur have been great partners, colleagues, and friends over the years that we have built the *Career-Leader* program. I am excited about the work that lies ahead of us.

From Beijing, Chicago, and Singapore, to Barcelona, Cambridge, and Lausanne, and from many other cities around the world, over a thousand counselors, professors, and career services professionals have sponsored or participated in the workshops on counseling and self-assessment that my colleagues and I have taught. I thank them all for their enthusiasm, ideas, friendship, and dedication to their students.

I want to thank Kris Dahl, my agent at ICM, for taking on this, our third project together.

A special thanks goes to Melinda Merino at Harvard Business School Press, who championed this project from the beginning and saw it through its many phases. Julia Ely has worked diligently during the production process. Rick Ruback, Linda Butler, Laura Nash, Fran Davis, Pam Lassiter, Jim Waldroop, and an anonymous reviewer read early drafts and provided valuable suggestions and encouragement. Connie Hale's editorial contributions have been truly extraordinary. Her enthusiasm, talent, and persistence have made this a much more accessible (and much shorter) book. Andrea Truax's careful and quick typing saved the day when deadlines loomed, and Pam Goett provided thoughtful and detailed copy editing. Jennifer Waring skillfully guided this project through the production process.

As always, I am full of gratitude for my wife Linda's patience, insight, and unwavering support.

In 1995, Betsy Sloan was thirty-five years old and had worked her way into "the perfect job." As a CPA in a large California insurance company, she had a great salary, stock options, a "fabulous boss," and hours that were the envy of her friends.

"And I was miserable," she says today. She leans comfortably into the back of a chair, her dark eyes sharply focused behind her stylish, orange-framed glasses. "The art of the deal, the big transaction—that never did it for me. What was worse, I could project thirty years into the future and know exactly what I'd be doing every quarter—making SEC filings, doing internal reporting for the CFO. It was mind-numbing."

"I felt totally stuck," she adds. "I made too much money to quit, but I hated not being able to do what I really wanted."

Betsy had never been encouraged to "do what she really wanted." Her middle-class, suburban family had urged her to develop strong skills and then find a job that would set her up for life. Always good at pleasing teachers, parents, and professors, she'd earned a 4.0 average in high school, won a full scholarship to college, excelled in accounting, and landed a job in a "Big Eight" CPA firm. After six years, she moved to the dream job at the insurance company.

Then one day she decided she couldn't do it anymore. She quit and left the office—and its financial security—the very same day. Betsy moved in with her parents and started taking classes at the local community college. One of those classes was creative writing. "I started writing about what I loved," she recalls. "I realized that I had been happiest in my life when I was in school. I loved that environment. Actually, I'd always secretly wanted to be a teacher. So I took the subject-matter proficiency classes to be a math teacher, and then I applied to graduate school for a master's in education."

By the time she turned thirty-eight, Betsy was teaching ninth-grade algebra and pre-calculus honors at a Seattle public high school. She had gone from making $106,000 a year to making $34,000. And she was loving every minute of it.

All of us, like Betsy, can suddenly find ourselves stuck and miserable. These feelings might come at predictable moments: with the loss of a job; the end of a romance; the departure of a child and the sudden yawning of an empty nest; or the death of someone who has long helped us feel recognized, loved, and appreciated. But they might also come at unpredictable moments: when the job of a lifetime somehow loses its juice; when we ache for intimacy but can't seem to find the right partner; when we find ourselves longing to renew a sense of life's adventure.

At these moments, we find ourselves at an impasse, and we suffer. At work we feel stale or unchallenged—or fret that we are not progressing to a more rewarding role. In our personal lives we feel agitated, deflated, or downright bored. We are desperate to discover a meaningful way to contribute at work, to find a reinvigorated role in our families, and to dive back into the current of our own lives. We sense that life is flowing all around us, but we sit like a boulder in a river, yearning to be swept along and transformed by the river's great energy.

The experience of being carried off by this energy is the surge of life, a time when our ideas and the will to act on them come from a well deeper than our own small selves. We feel connected; we get things done; we sense something exciting is at hand. We are, as the psychologist Mihaly Csikszentmihalyi would say, "in the flow."

When we are at an impasse, we often cannot even sense this flow—or see how close we are to a dynamic dislodging that would place us back into the energy of the moving current. When we are feeling stuck, we forget that the next thing that will wake us up and energize us deeply is already in motion upstream, moving toward our awareness. When we have run aground, we sometimes fail to realize that this is a *necessary* crisis; without it we cannot grow, change, and—eventually—live more fully in a larger world.

Impasse and Vision

This is a book about how impasse, like the Greek god Hermes, often appears in our lives as a herald, to let us know we must change. But it is also about vision. It is about how we find our way, again and again, from impasse to renewed meaning—at work, at home, with colleagues, and with family—and how we find a renewed sense of self in those aspects of our lives that bring both passion and satisfaction.

Vision, as I use the word here, is not merely a plan for the future, it also is a renewed sense of purpose in our day-to-day work. It entails stopping, reflecting, imagining, and then acting—stepping anew into the creative flow. It requires building, over time, a clearer and more immediate awareness of the activities, people, and environments we are most likely to find rewarding. Vision allows us to tap into what is already moving within us at a deeper level, already asking for fuller expression. With vision, we are better able to recognize what resources, behavior changes, and relationships we will need in order to reconnect with what is most important to us.

When we have a clear vision, we feel more connected to the world, more alive. The gap between our thought and action, our internal world and external world, vanishes, and we more fully occupy our "self." Our everyday choices feed off our vision the way a lantern flame feeds off kerosene.

Just as important as vision is *re-vision*, because the process of seeing anew happens time and again throughout our lives. Sometimes re-vision leads to a relatively minor decision, as when we plan carefully for an important event or change the priorities of certain tasks. At other times, re-vision leads us to major change, as when we marry or pursue a radically new career path. There are times of great epiphanies, when our awareness opens and we gain insight into what big things we want and which big things we must do. And then there are times when a slight shift makes a dramatic difference in how we feel about something smaller—the arc of our workday or our time with our children.

Missed Opportunities: Staying Stuck

The shock of the experiencing crisis and impasse—the heralds of the need for a new vision—can overwhelm us. The old issues and the memories they evoke can seem so painful that we suppress them or disassociate from them before they even become conscious. We may choose, with or without full awareness, to retreat or to evade. "Just let me get through this so I can get back to what I was doing," we might tell ourselves, or "I know this needs my attention, but I just can't face it right now." This response is not a sign of moral

FIGURE I-1

Staying stuck

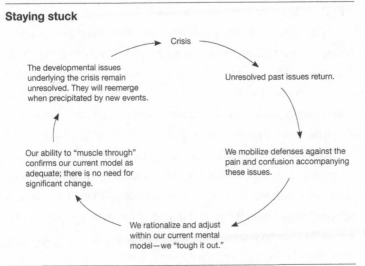

weakness—sometimes what life presents is just too much. And staying stuck may seem like the most natural way to move forward because it allows us to hew the familiar, to remain "who we are"— or who we think we must be. But while defensive evasion may get us past the immediate circumstances of the crisis, it simply postpones resolving the issue underlying the crisis, and going through change. There is no integration of the crisis experience, as demonstrated in figure I-1.

The Cycle of Impasse

If we are to make real change, there is a predictable "cycle of impasse" we all must go through and a pattern to the way we can move toward clarity and a renewed sense of vision. The impasse cycle—in which we move from feeling deeply stuck to gradually imagining a new place in life and taking the leap to get there—has six predictable phases.

In the first phase the crisis develops. Something in the way in which we order life and move through it is no longer working. Crisis may arrive with a painful event: a serious illness, the death of a loved one, or a financial setback. It may arrive in the subtle symptoms of unrest, anxiety, or boredom. Our usual sense of certainty disappears. We begin to see that something is missing. We long for change.

The crisis deepens in the second phase. Our attempts to avoid, rationalize, and evade have not worked, and things are getting worse. Even more difficult, this crisis is starting to feel familiar. It brings difficult feelings from the past. "I thought I was done with all of that," we say; but our feelings of resentment or inadequacy or shame continue. We stop trying to rationalize or evade the reality of the crisis and acknowledge that we cannot continue business as usual. Our old way of doing things, our comfortable routines, are no longer working—and we know it. The crisis has shown that our familiar "model" for the way life works is inadequate.

In phase three that old model completely breaks up and we hit bottom, drop our defenses, and open up. It is impossible to deny that our wheels are deep in the mud, so we get out of the car, stand there, and begin to listen to the sounds of the night around us. What can we possibly do to get unstuck?

This coming to a compete halt, this admission that we are beyond our resources, this opening up, is the very condition that makes phase four possible. Now we can receive not only new information, but also a new *type* of information that comes not in the form of fantasy, but of real imagination. We begin to receive coded images of what is missing in our lives, we notice signs pointing to what needs to happen next. The work to be done at this phase is the work of disciplined imagination, which allows our understanding to shift. We find ourselves using a mode of thinking that is less linear and more metaphorical. We recognize new relationships between forces and ideas that previously seemed in opposition. Our perspective becomes less certain and dogmatic, more pliable and full of possibilities. We begin to catch sight of something new on the horizon.

As we begin to emerge from the crisis, we take stock of the experience itself and how it has affected us. We realize that the pain of the impasse experience has taught us, in an immediate way, what counts and what doesn't. We learn something vital about what we need and want, and about what we are willing to give up to get these things. We may be shaken, but at the same time our feet seem a little more firmly planted in the earth. Phase five marks an opportunity for a deeper reflection on what our choices have shown us about who we are. And with each journey through the impasse cycle, our mental model of the world and our place in it shifts, and we acquire a surer appreciation of our unique identity. We gain a clearer sense of what works for us and what doesn't. And we develop better instincts—and greater confidence—about how to find the right path, about how to grow and contribute to the lives around us. We can more easily identify the types of work, the people, and the environments that will fulfill us the most.

But our lives do not change without action. The impasse crisis has its resolution in a decision to make specific choices that change our day-to-day reality. The final, sixth phase of the impasse cycle may be a decision to confront a coworker, to begin work on a book, to go to graduate school, to end a relationship, or to move to the country. The decision might also be as simple as a change in a daily schedule or a commitment to balancing bank accounts monthly.

Knowing what the action needs to be, and actually performing it, is what seals the cycle of learning and change and allows us to move forward.

If we move through each of the six phases with all of the honesty and energy we can muster, we have an opportunity to break through the limitations we had unconsciously placed on ourselves and exceed previous notions of what we might do with what we have been given. Impasses will come again—crisis is the crucible for the work of making a larger self—but the next time we can meet the crisis with all that we gained from previous work. The next cycle will take place at a higher level of integration, as our life experience widens and we live with a self that is more tolerant, less self-critical, and more ready to accept aspects of our own personhood that had been either unrecognized or exiled. Figure I-2 provides a visual overview of the process.

The body of this book will guide you through the entire process, with these distinct phases:

- The arrival of the crisis and impasse (chapter 1)

- Its deepening and the attendant reemergence of unresolved issues (chapter 2)

- The dropping of old assumptions and the opening up to new information (chapter 3)

- The shift to a new way of understanding our situation (chapter 4)

- The greater recognition of deep patterns of our personality (chapters 5, 6, 7, and 8)

- The decision to take concrete action (chapters 9 and 10).

This is the process that leads to a larger sense of the world and our place in it.

FIGURE I-2

Getting unstuck: the cycle of impasse and vision

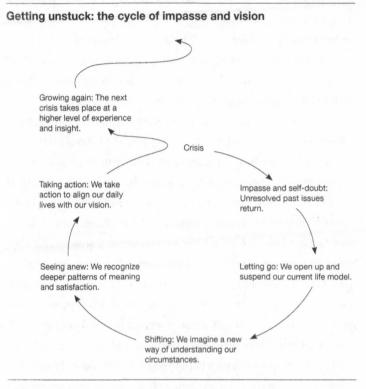

Growing again: The next crisis takes place at a higher level of experience and insight.

Crisis

Taking action: We take action to align our daily lives with our vision.

Impasse and self-doubt: Unresolved past issues return.

Seeing anew: We recognize deeper patterns of meaning and satisfaction.

Letting go: We open up and suspend our current life model.

Shifting: We imagine a new way of understanding our circumstances.

My Perspective

My understanding of what we experience when we are stuck, and how we can get ourselves unstuck, has evolved out of more than thirty years of work as a social scientist, psychotherapist, and career counselor. I have worked at Harvard Business School and with people from a variety of organizations, from small startups to *Fortune* 500 corporations, as well as with individual executives during times of career transition. Some people have come to me when they have been let go or told that termination is imminent;

others seek my counsel because they lack a sense of accomplishment in an otherwise stable and lucrative job or because they want to find more rewarding work. Whether consciously or not, they all come looking for meaning. As a result, I have focused much of my research on the "meaning of meaning"—on how individuals find a path to life situations that are satisfying and sustainable.

I am also a teacher of other counselors and mentors. At Harvard, I direct a counseling and coaching program, and I travel around the world to train coaches and counselors at other universities.

In addition to my work on the Harvard Business School faculty as a writer and researcher, I direct a career development program designed to help MBA students develop a vision of their career. When they first set foot on campus, the vast majority of students, at Harvard and elsewhere, lack a clear idea of what they want do with their lives. In fact, many enroll in an MBA program as the first step in finding their future. These students, during two short years in school, must discover how they differ from every other member of the class and how that will help them make the most of the career ahead.

I approach my work with both executives and students with two different but complementary perspectives. First, I am researcher using large databases and sophisticated quantitative analyses to study the way in which personality structure is related to job choice and career satisfaction. My databases now have psychological testing information on more than 150,000 business professionals and MBA students. This research has led to a number of theoretical models and psychological tests that I use in my teaching, mentoring, and counseling.

But I am not just a social scientist; I am also a psychotherapist. My second perspective, then, is that of mentor for the many students and clients who have worked with me personally as they

faced their own crises and impasses. It is from the chair in my counseling office that I have learned the most about how people come to
a vision of what they want their lives to be and about how they make
the bold choices to make that vision real.

How to Use This Book

This book is not about these business executives, these students, or these particular clients. It is about you and the work you
must do, many times in the course of your life, to move closer to
more meaningful work and a more meaningful life.

You will be using the vision-building exercises I use in my classes
at Harvard and in my workshops with executives and career coaches
all over the world. Specifically, you will:

- Learn how to recognize the state of psychological impasse
  and use it as the starting point for real change in the way
  you make life and work choices;

- Participate in exercises that activate, evoke, and deepen
  images that will shape your new life vision;

- Learn how to recognize enduring patterns of meaning that
  point to the activities, rewards, types of people, work cultures, and communities that are most likely to satisfy you;

- Learn how the creative work you do at times of impasse can
  enable you to take action and make life choices that will
  make your vision a reality.

I emphasize career and work crises, but impasse does not differentiate between the work life and the personal life. This approach

is relevant for anyone who has come to realize that something must change—in a job description, in working habits, in a marriage, in a friendship, or in an overly frenetic and frustrating way of living. Even though you have picked up this book, your reasons for doing so may not yet be fully formed or understood. That is a good place to begin—that vague sense of possibility will have the chance to emerge as you move deeper into the way of working that this book presents.

A brief note on the theoretical underpinnings of this material: this book does not offer new developmental theory, although it calls repeatedly on theory to help us look deeper into what is actually going on during a time of impasse. To this end, it will use both the theory and models that have emerged from my own research and from the work of some of the most prominent developmental psychologists of the past century. If you are interested in the potent ideas of these researchers and psychotherapists, you will find references in the notes section and in the annotated bibliography in appendix A.

More important than some schema of adult development, however, is the actual experience of working through psychological impasse. Each phase of the impasse cycle and vision process has its own mood and its own challenges. Each requires its own response. This is not about speed-reading or quick course corrections. There will be times to be still and listen, even when you want to run. There will be times to let your sensibilities sink deeper until you reach a bottom that can support a new movement upward. There will times to be busy, to focus and work as if your life depended on it. It is important to sense the mood, gauge the challenge, and calibrate the response appropriate for each phase.

The book is designed as a journey; you will move through a sequence of meditations, readings, and exercises designed to take you through the full impasse cycle and into a richer vision of your work and life. The best way to get unstuck is to take your time with the book, and to work through each exercise as it appears in the text. Of course, you may want to do some exercises more than once during this journey—and again and again in the future when the feeling of impasse returns.

Betsy's Vision

"I've always liked math, but it's sharing the ideas with students that gets me out of bed in the morning," says Betsy Sloan, reflecting on her former career as a CPA and her current life as a teacher. "I care more about people than the bottom line. And I really care about ninth-graders: you get to fall in love with them and then have them for three more years."

As a high-school teacher, Betsy has found the freedom to be who she really is. "As a CPA in a Big Eight firm in the 1980s," she says, "I couldn't wear pants. I couldn't even wear a *dress*. It had to be a suit. In the insurance firm in the 1990s *maybe* I could wear a pants suit." Her work attire today is a brown button-down blouse and khaki trousers, and her auburn hair falls to her shoulders in graceful waves. But during her nine years as a teacher she's gone from her natural auburn to black to blonde—and back to auburn.

"Students are very accepting," she says. "All they care about is how much homework I give them. And all the administration cares about is whether I'm teaching the curriculum."

"What *I* care about is that the kids get my jokes," she adds, laughing. "I'm shy, but put me in front of a class and I'm a ham."

Quickly settling into a more reflective tone she adds, "My charge is much more than developing good math students." Betsy has found

DEEP DIVE

Using This Book

This book is practical. It is meant to be used. It will lead you through the process I use with students at the Harvard Business School and with participants in my workshops. The chapters will lead you in sequence through the six phases of the vision cycle: The arrival of the *crisis*, the *deepening* of the crisis, *letting go* of your current mental model, making a crucial *shift* to a new perspective, *recognizing* the deep *patterns* of your personality, and *taking action* for meaningful change.

Throughout the book, there are highlighted self-assessment Deep Dive exercises. These exercises allow you to take the material you have just read and focus it immediately and specifically on your own life situation. I encourage you to participate in the One Hundred Jobs exercise presented in chapter 4 as it will provide an

that the great meaning in her work comes from counseling and mentoring her students, whether leading a discussion after one student died in a car accident or inviting kids into her classroom at lunchtime. "We usually have four games of Scrabble going, kids hanging out over Scrabble and talking."

For those of us who, like Betsy, take the time to fully experience impasse—letting the crisis deepen, listening to that clear inner voice, and taking action to make change—life will prove more and challenging than our younger selves had imagined, and it will, at the same time, feel more familiar and authentic.

experiential basis for many of the ideas discussed in later chapters. A second major exercise, the *Image Gathering* exercise also introduced in chapter 4, is actually a guided meditation, and you may listen to me presenting this exercise by going to www.careerleader .com/gettingunstuck. This Web site will also provide additional material for applying the ideas presented in this book to your work and life situation. Completing the *Image Gathering* exercise is not essential for using this book, but it will add richness and texture to the insights you gain from the One Hundred Jobs exercise. For each of these exercises, there are detailed guidance and case examples.

You may, of course, skip the exercises altogether and read the book for the theory it presents. There are many stories and case histories to help bring the ideas to life as you do so. However, I extend an invitation now, as you begin the book, to enter into the reading as fully as possible and make it an experience of your own frontier.

I wrote this book to guide you through the necessary crisis of growth that each experience at impasse brings. (See "Deep Dive: Using This Book.") It is my hope that what I have learned about how this process takes place will draw you deeper into your own vision for what needs to come next in life and deeper, as well, into your ability to recognize and help those around you who find themselves at their own frontiers.

PART I

Impasse

*Faced with a crisis at work or in our personal life, we
try to push our way forward using our old views and
methods. Soon we realize this is not working and find
ourselves at a dead end. Energy and inspiration begin
to evaporate; our conviction seems less certain. We
begin to hear the stinging voice of our inner critic and
old doubts about our ability and our direction return.
We seem to be both sinking and moving backward.
These feelings at first may bring alarm, but we must
come to recognize them as signals that an important
process is beginning. Being at impasse is a developmental necessity. It can lead to a new way of understanding and a new type of information. We have
arrived at an important frontier.*

ONE

Facing Crisis

I T WAS AN AFTERNOON in late spring, a few weeks before her graduation from the Sloan School of Management
at MIT, and Marcy Kaufman was feeling unsettled.[1] Sitting in my office, she leaned forward in her chair, her short blonde hair framing an
alert expression and a direct gaze. I knew this alertness well, and
how it could change in a moment from pensive reflection to a mis-
chievous smile. But today her look was more serious; she wanted to
know if she could continue counseling with me after graduation.

Marcy was no stranger to big changes or unsettling times.
Bright, athletic, and full of energy, she had a history of taking things
straight on. She grew up in Los Angeles, the only girl in a family of
sports-oriented boys. Her brothers admired her tomboy toughness
and let her into their rough-and-tumble crowd. When high school
became boring, she arranged to graduate early, at sixteen, and spend

six months traveling alone on a bus tour of Africa. At eighteen she enrolled at California Institute of Technology and majored in computer science. She excelled on all fronts. At five feet ten inches tall, she was a standout on the basketball team. She was also a star student and maintained a wide circle of friends. In business graduate school, she enjoyed her classes, her summer internship, and her time with her classmates.

Now twenty-seven, she had arrived at a place that, at least for the moment, seemed far less certain. She had a boyfriend, Henry, but it was not clear just where that stop-and-go relationship was headed. He was working in New England and so, for the time being, she planned to stay in the greater Boston area. But doing what? Marcy had come to MIT because leadership seemed to be her destiny, but, as for many of her fellow students, the best path toward that destiny was not clear. The job market was good, but as Marcy went from interview to interview she was not sure what she was trying to accomplish. Was she looking for the best job or the least bad job that would allow her to stay with Henry? She was no longer a software engineer, but what then was she?

My clients, unique as they are, all come to me for the same reason: they are stuck. They are uncertain about what to do to move closer to a more fulfilling work or life situation. Marcy was at such an impasse. She had "come to the end of her thinking," and found herself at an uncomfortable crossroads. She felt torn between following her classmates in pursuing high-paying jobs in prestigious firms and her desire to make the relationship with Henry work. Beneath this tension was another source of stress that was even more unsettling, in that it was far more vague and harder to describe. It was more a feeling in the pit of her stomach than a problem that she could formulate and bring to a counselor.

What I as a career counselor and psychotherapist could see, but

Marcy could not, is that as we live our lives, things don't happen in a straight line, a little bit at a time, day by day. Growth as a person does not occur in a predictable and sequential fashion. Many times a path comes to an abrupt halt, only to continue again at a different place, at a different level. Our lives unfold more like that of the caterpillar and butterfly than we are perhaps ready to acknowledge. An impasse like Marcy's was the first step in changing her very idea about what she really wanted and about how happiness might come into her world.

To understand this, it can be helpful to think of the worlds we inhabited as seven-year-olds and as seventeen-year-olds. Our lives in our second decade are not continuations of our childhood in a bigger body, but are different altogether. The transition to adolescence brought with it a crisis; the seven-year-old's way of finding happiness in the world simply no longer worked. With struggle, we were able to forge a whole new perspective and a whole new agenda. The lines of our childhood worlds were broken, and new lines began at a very different place on the page. And this sense of disjunction and radical change happens again and again. When we talk about a childhood and adolescence and adulthood, or about Picasso in his Rose Period and then in his Blue Period, or about the early recordings of Miles Davis and then his last, in a real sense we are talking about almost different characters in each case. The change has been that radical and the life being experienced is that different.

In recent decades, developmental psychologists have created highly useful theoretical models of these necessary disjunctures in human development.[2] Our concern here, however, is not theoretical. What does it mean to be, like Marcy, at the very point of the break? How do we find a new line of travel? If we simply try our old ways of understanding, it becomes painfully clear that the crisis is deepening.

The Black Sun

Both Greek and Celtic mythology include a mysterious image known as the "Black Sun," which can be visualized as tremendous energy radiating from a dense and dark center. (Celtic myths sometimes place it in the center of the earth.) And it stands in contrast to the metaphoric qualities we commonly associate with the sun: The brightness of day gives life its warmth. Good things must be close by when we rise to a sunny morning.

But the idea behind the ancient Black Sun image is that energy and life radiate from darkness as well. Some kinds of energy that we need for growth and for a complete life come only from the experience of darkness. This Black Sun is a hidden resource, a font of energy that is available if we recognize it for what it is and know how to turn toward it and accept it. Being dark, its energy is hidden. We cannot explain it in the same way we can explain things in the light of the more familiar sun. The wisdom and energy it brings are less obvious, less rational.

Myths illuminate subtle aspects of the human condition and human development. The Black Sun tells us that there is value in slowing down and being patient when things seem dark and unclear. Do not run from such experiences, it says. Turn toward the difficult time. By just focusing on it and sticking with it we will discover power that radiates from it as surely as warming light radiates from the daytime sun.

The Black Sun is an apt metaphor for the deep concentration and inward focus that precedes the actual act of writing the poem, founding the company, forming the sculpture, or jumping into a radically different role at work. In all of these cases, we do not operate "in the light" or "from the light"; instead, we are going where we have not been before and are trusting an intuition that seems to rise from the depths of our selves. The successful artist and the successful businessperson alike learn how to stay with this process of being stuck in the darkness; in fact, they stick with it until a new momentum emerges from the very experience of being stuck, of being in the dark.

The problem, of course, is that we are afraid of the dark. We want to move in the sunshine, walk along familiar streets, and have experiences that are sure to give us pleasure. We want to feel that most of life can be planned and that we have a reasonable chance of avoiding pain. The idea of staying with things just as they are, without a plan, of suspending our model of how things work, puts us at a frontier of unknowing, which is to say at a place that is "dark" to our previous conception of things, to our plan for ourselves and our notion of how everything works. We avoid this dim frontier, and so we stay stuck.

Being in the dark, at an impasse, is not clinical depression. (It is important to know the difference, though; appendix B describes how to differentiate the two.) Sometimes we can't help seeing impasse as failure, rather than as a necessary crisis in the service of larger creative movement. There is a danger of internalizing the experience of impasse as evidence of personal deficiency, as a statement about our self-worth. This can be painful. We may need the help of a friend, coach, or counselor to reflect the reality of the situation back to us and remind us that this is tough time and not a statement about who we are in the core of our being.

Impasse

When Marcy started to see me regularly after her graduation, she was not depressed in the clinical sense of the term. Her world, however, did seem flat rather than round and full. She sensed something was missing, and this feeling was all the more pronounced because she had always experienced life rushing forward, and had always known great confidence and youthful vitality.

Marcy had accepted a job in sales, an unusual choice for Sloan graduates, who more often choose positions in professional services firms or corporations that call on the strategic skills taught in the MBA curriculum. Marcy was ambivalent about her choice. She was working for a relatively small company that provided professional employees, mostly information technology specialists, on a temporary basis. She was going on the road regionally to analyze the computer programming and computer support employment needs of potential clients. She was the only woman on the sales force, but this in itself was neither new nor daunting. In fact, Marcy enjoyed the "one of the guys" camaraderie; it reminded her of times with her undergraduate buddies at their fraternity and of hanging out with her brothers before that. No, the problem was that she just wasn't very excited generally and could not see how this work would take her toward the management roles she had envisioned when she applied to MIT.

The most creative people I know have learned, over time, to feel more at home during these times of impasse. Not that they *like* the experience of feeling slowed down or stuck; like all of us they enjoy the thrill of being in motion on a new project or venture. But they no longer expend energy in *avoiding* the experience of impasse and, most important, they no longer *fear* this experience. They have cultivated a capability to experience darker and heavier times as part of a larger cycle of creativity and change. They no longer identify with impasse; they are able to say, "This condition, this feeling state is "something I am going through," rather than "something I am."

But most of us, like Marcy, have not learned how to turn toward the Black Sun and realize the energy that is latent in times of crisis and impasse. We leave that to the poet, painter, or songwriter. (See Deep Dive: The Feeling of Impasse.)

My sessions with Marcy, alternating between career questions and uncertainties she had about her relationship with Henry, began

DEEP DIVE

The Feeling of Impasse

This first Deep Dive presents us with a paradox. Deep Dive sections are the "to do" part of the book. When you first find yourself in impasse, however, there is no "to-do." Not yet. In fact, the impasse process does not begin until you stop "doing" the things that we all do to keep the feelings of impasse at bay. We all try to get away from the feelings of being stuck and sinking. Nevertheless, just allowing yourself to accept them is the first step. Not-doing is the first "to-do."

But you might pay attention to those thoughts, images, memories, and feelings that crop up as you read this chapter. You have been at impasse before. You know this experience of coming to a stop, this feeling of emotional flatness, and this sense of no direction. Allow these thoughts, images, memories, and feelings to arise, develop, and then go wherever they may go. Attend to this emotional climate of impasse in a personal way now, and then continue to read on. You can return to this step in the process at any time.

to turn her toward the uncertainties of her Black Sun period of change. Between talk of career and relationship, as she let herself drop down into the experience of impasse, Marcy shared something else: her father was dying of cancer. I was more interested in this than she. She would grow quiet when we turned to this topic. It was not as if she were actively avoiding talking about her father, it was just that she did not have words for it. She was not in denial; she was just stuck. Her father, a computer scientist himself, was clearly an important person for her. She had a good relationship with him, but the emotionally conservative culture of her childhood had not provided her with much of a vocabulary to reexperience it for herself or convey her experience. I sensed that Marcy's relationship with her father was an important part of her impasse.

Images of "Stuck"

When we find ourselves at impasse, we all begin to tell a story that explains our sense of being stuck or lost. It is as if, at some level, we know that our explanation of things is not working, so we review it and try one more time to make it work. If we seek out friends or counselors, we create the latest version of that explanation, of that "story" in front of them.

But we also come bearing information about ourselves that is pre-cognition, pre-language, and pre-story. And it is that information we need next. This information comes from close to the core of our beings and presents itself first as a sense that something is amiss and we must figure out what it is. It is something that is not buried deeply but is seemingly poised right at the edge of our awareness. It is a feeling in the gut not so different from trying to remember the name of someone you recently met. The name is there but you just can't grasp it. This information is what philosopher and psychologist Eugene Gendlin calls the *implicit*.[3]

What we know implicitly about a current situation, and about what we need to do next to live more fully, comes to us first through our body, through a vague, intuitive "hunch," through tentative or unformed thoughts, or through our feelings. This implicit apprehension is not yet at a level of awareness where we can fully recognize it and use it. In order to take hold of the implicit we must develop it into the next level of awareness; it must become *image*.

An image is a cognitive representation—it might be visual (a picture), it might be physical (a sensation), it might be emotional (a feeling), it might be intuitive (a nascent thought). It is the first glimpse of a part of our reality that has been just beyond our reach. It may arrive spontaneously on canvas or as an impulse that opens up into a phrase as we write. It is the first recognition that there is an aspect of our experience we have yet to fully own, yet to put into the language that would allow us to pick it up and know it as a real part of our life. Any real vision that can lead us forward can only be built upon and first experienced through images.

For Marcy, the image came in a dream.

I'm walking on a trail through the woods, along the edge of a large lake. I am very tired; I have been walking for a long time. It is autumn and late afternoon; I am alone. I notice that a car is coming slowly down a narrow dirt road through the woods toward me. As it comes closer I see that it is a brand new, brightly shining, cherry-red minivan. It stops near me and I walk over to it. The door opens and I climb into the large front seat on the passenger side and, exhausted, settle back comfortably.

The driver turns to me. He is my father.

Once such an image emerges, we struggle to make sense of our new imagination and where it may realistically lead us. The first task is to extract key themes, the "code" of the emerging vision. Next, the emerging images, themes, and dynamic tensions need to be "amplified," or described in a fully extended way. A new picture develops, sometimes surpassing our ability to find words to describe it. But as we amplify the image, it may reveal aspects of our situation that are conflicted, paradoxical, or disturbing, but which, at the same time, present a fuller picture of our situation and a fuller picture of what needs to be acted upon.

This amplification may be initiated by a perceptive friend or a professional counselor who probes and challenges our new responses; over time we can ourselves develop the skill to follow images to their wider meaning.

In Marcy's dream, the images seemed to be right there, some more important than others. Marcy's hyperachieving childhood was there in that young hiker's fatigue and sense of loneliness, that long walk along the edge of those wide waters. But I wanted to know about that cherry-red van.

"I find my attention drawn to the van." I said, "Can you see it in your mind's eye?"

"Yes."

"Look at it, hold your attention there. What is happening?"

"It is big, very big. I am walking toward it."

"How are you feeling?" I inquired softly.

Marcy was silent.

"How does its bigness make you feel?" I pressed on.

"Safe, it makes me feel safe. I am relieved," she answered, her voice soft.

"It is big and it is red," I said, encouraging her to stay with the image. "Just pay attention."

Marcy's eyes began to well up with tears. Here was her father again when she, exhausted and tired of this traveling, needed him. He was big and strong and, even if silent in the driver's seat, full of a quiet, unstated, but impossible-to-miss love. The image of the dream was presenting a reality for which neither Marcy nor her father yet had words.

Marcy chose a very direct way to take what she had learned from our work with imagery into her life. Her father was ill and bedridden. During her next visit to him, she told him her dream, and she told him what the dream meant for her. She thanked him for being that big, strong, and warm presence for her, for always being there to come back to from her adventures and travels. His presence, at home and in the background, was a hitherto unacknowledged base from which she could venture out and take the risks that had led to her remarkable achievements.

These things needed to be understood and spoken. For Marcy, big adventures lay ahead—possibly marriage and a career path that would lead her away from the explorations of her twenties into the commitments of full adulthood. It was now sinking in that there would no longer be a paternal support van following her on these journeys. It would be ever more important that she acknowledge the meaning of her father's presence, and take the gift of that presence inside herself for help during those times ahead when her hike might again seem tiring or lonely.

Marcy's working through of what she needed in order to say goodbye to her father seemed to open up other parts of her life.

What she had originally seen as issues involving job choice and a relationship she now saw in the larger context of a leave-taking; she was exiting her young adulthood with its deep roots in the emotional bonds of childhood and adolescence.

Having grasped the underlying source of her impasse, she was ready to act. She and Henry decided to marry, and they moved to Atlanta where more substantial jobs were available for both.

Once impasse is understood as a necessary crisis, it is possible to look at such tough times as opportunities to make choices that reclaim meaning in our daily lives. Marcy's father's impending death brought her to a point that literally stopped her, though she was not aware of what was happening at the time. But his dying actually brought her to a threshold that she had to move through to grow up and step more deeply into life's currents.

Before we take up the work of deepening our imagination, we must look more closely at the impasse experience. A life impasse fulfills a specific purpose in our psychological development. It is a call to return to and integrate aspects of our emotional and psychological being that have been set aside because of competing life circumstances. In the next chapter we see how as an impasse deepens, it brings with it unresolved issues from our past.

TWO

Feeling Stuck and
Doubting Ourselves

R AYMOND BECKER has curly graying hair; he is short, with a compact, athletic build. Handsome, outgoing, and affable, he has a quick wit, a ready smile, and an engaging manner. His mobile face would doom him to defeat in any serious game of poker. He creates the impression of an electrical charge in a perpetual state of overflow, as if the voltage passing through his system is always exceeding the capacity of his nervous-system wiring. He never sits quietly in a chair, but rather shifts and leans, crossing and uncrossing his legs, in a restless attempt to make peace with a piece of furniture that seems designed to trap rather than support him. He speaks rapidly as he shifts and gestures, his speech pressured by the intensity of his ideas and by his urgent desire to be heard.

I have known Raymond for well over a decade, since he was an MBA student at Dartmouth's Tuck School of Business. He has come to me for counsel in the intervening years as he has built a successful, though often rocky, career as a manager in large real estate development companies. Raymond, who grew up in an affluent Chicago suburb, comes from an intellectual, competitive, and ambitious family. His father has had a very successful career in medicine, and his older brother started two companies before the age of thirty. In our counseling sessions, Raymond would tell stories of the family dinner table conversations, where lightning-quick repartee was necessary simply to hold one's own. Throughout his adolescence and adulthood, Raymond has reenacted the scene of having to hold his own among smart, ambitious peers. Engaging in competitive repartee has become his way of gaining recognition. Every board meeting and every strategy session of his company's business development group become for him one more dinner gathering. He often feels threatened that he will be totally eclipsed by the current stand-in for his brilliant brother.

Most objective observers would say that Raymond's career has been more successful than that of his brother. But even as his brother's business was failing and Raymond was gaining a reputation in his field, Raymond was only intermittently able to see that he was not the awkward fifteen-year-old tripped up one more time by the wit of his far more sophisticated seventeen-year-old sibling. And, as is often true with all attempts at psychological change, Raymond's awareness of his own relative success, and his insight into the dynamics of his sibling rivalry, have not ended his feelings of inadequacy.

This painful pattern has brought Raymond back to my office several times over the years during times of career impasse. Each crisis has also brought him back to the work of separating what is truly satisfying to him from the compulsive need to hyperaccomplish and to establish, once and for all, his "place at the table." Each crisis is saying to him: "Here, this has not worked out. Try once again to work on what really counts for you, not for that adolescent who so desperately wants recognition." It has taken working through several professional crises, each bringing a painful sense of inadequacy, for Raymond to begin to break free from his adolescent self.

Like Raymond, each of us must wrestle the constraints of past roles. These cause impasse as much as any challenges in our current environment. We seldom realize this at the outset of the crisis; most of the time it seems to be coming from "out there." Then as a crisis turns to impasse, we begin to realize that the past is not just something that happened a long time ago.

The Hold of the Past

Psychoanalyst Erik Erikson described human development as "epigenetic": we grow outward around the edges of our younger selves, like a tree's annual growth rings. We carry forward both our strengths and our wounds, and the latter can get in the way—especially when we deny them. To escape the hold of the past, we must first perceive what we carry from it. Impasse offers us an opportunity to revisit earlier fears and bring them into the light of day. In Raymond's case, the impasse had to deepen before he could see how a self-image founded on earlier experiences of inadequacy is a great burden. Self-images often seem to have lives of their own, separate from our daily reality, and they exert a powerful presence that affects decisions and distorts perceptions. These distortions lead us away from the ability to pursue the work and the relationships that hold the greatest promise for fulfillment.

Like Raymond, we all find a part of us that resists the notion that things must change. Ego, which wants to keep everything familiar, is terrified of losing itself, not to mention the old patterns and conditioned habits that prop it up. The first sense that we might be something other than the person we thought we were is always unsettling. Ego insists that there are indeed experiences to fear, and ego justifies our defenses.

Ghosts from the past haunt a time of impasse. They may not choose to speak or even show themselves in a recognizable form. They may instead appear as a depressed mood, increased irritability, a lingering sense of ennui, or a disassociated sense of being "spaced out" and unable to focus on the action that life demands. They may manifest as unbidden memories of critical figures from the past: a father who expected greater athletic prowess or a mother who could not find praise for a "B" no matter how hard we had worked for it. They may come disguised, as they did for Raymond, as images of an earlier, less mature, and less confident self that we have long since transcended. Like Raymond, we may once more trot out the fearful child or conflicted adolescent.

Sometimes ghosts appear as pure, unspecified fear—a free-floating anxiety that we cannot connect to any particular threat. This return of the past is the essence of the second phase of impasse. The return of old issues raises the emotional stakes of the crisis. It also brings us the opportunity, perhaps for the first time, to recognize the true nature of these specters, and bid them good-bye.

Ancestors

Karen Yamada first came to see me when she was thirty years old and had been in an engineering PhD program for several years. She had a complaint typical in academia: writer's block.

Karen's grandparents had come from Japan and settled in the Seattle area. Her grandfather worked as a laborer for a ship-supply company and later opened up a small hardware business. Her father expanded that business with a much wider line of products. He married Karen's mother at an early age, in a traditional Japanese ceremony attended by what was now an extended circle of family and friends who had themselves come from the old country. Later he purchased a home in the growing Japanese community.

World War II upended the family's prosperity and security. Forced to leave their home with only a few possessions, Karen's parents and grandparents lived out the war years in an internment camp. When they returned to Seattle in 1945, most of what they had built in America had vanished. So they built anew, becoming, after many years, successful small-business owners and householders once again. Karen was born years after the war, but she grew up in a community that held in its bones a sense of tentativeness. Members of that community knew that the passage of one or two generations gave few guarantees of acceptance into the mainstream.

Karen was born into a world of paradox. Her community still had its own doctors, lawyers, and community structure to protect it against anti-Japanese prejudices. But Karen's generation was expected to break into mainstream America, to find success and financial security while still keeping filial ties to the Japanese family, community, and customs.

This expectation was rarely spoken of directly. Karen absorbed it just by hearing the stories from the camps, stories of ongoing racial injustice, and stories about favorite sons and daughters. One message was that both security and a change for the better would accrue from acceptance into prestigious American colleges, and then positions in leading professional organizations.

Karen stepped naturally into this generational project. She excelled in school, and her family expected her to go far. She took accelerated courses in high school and then finished her undergraduate degree at Princeton in three years to save her family the tuition for a fourth year. She was a top performer in her first job with an engineering consulting firm. But after a few years, Karen sensed that something was missing. She had always enjoyed the classroom and was known as an effective tutor and mentor. A natural psychologist, she had a strong sense of personality differences and group dynamics. Fellow students, and later fellow workers, sought her out when conflicts arose with teachers, bosses, and colleagues. Karen decided that she wanted a role that would allow more of this interpersonal element. Eager to teach, she was accepted at an engineering doctoral program at Boston University.

Through all of her schooling and early employment, Karen had remained very close to her family and the Japanese community in Seattle. She fulfilled dutifully the traditional role of eldest daughter in her parents' home. She was present at traditional festivities and ceremonies. Her extended family and other community members spoke with pride of her accomplishments at Princeton and Boston University, but did not have any firsthand experience of what life was like in those settings or what it meant to belong to those communities simultaneously with their own. Karen was living in two worlds, and the strain of her dual citizenship was beginning to take its toll.

Karen was on a path leading further into the realm of elite professionals, as a senior manager in a technology firm or tenured professor at a major university. She was gradually joining the ranks of policymakers. She was leaving the world where disenfranchised immigrants hear on short notice that they must pack their belongings and leave their homes.

In our sessions, Karen was to learn how ambivalent she truly was about elitism. On the one hand, she admired her colleagues' intelligence and sense of privilege. She also admired the promise that a prestigious organization seemed to offer. On the other hand, she realized how little understanding her colleagues had of the world she came from, and of what it meant to feel truly vulnerable in a new country.

The bright, active hyperachiever seemed to be in perpetual argument with another less obvious internal figure. This figure seemed to be saying, "Slow down and really look at what you are doing." In our sessions we were to discover an even darker part of this message: "You are traitor. You are leaving your people behind. You are abandoning them. Stop now." She tended to experience writer's block and intermittent attacks of dissociation from her immediate experience when opportunities arose to advance her own interests by completing an important project, networking with a powerful person, or asserting herself in a conflict situation.

At first Karen had little insight into her symptoms, but then a dream presented a vivid picture of her impasse:

> I am at work in a new building at Boston University. Suddenly, I smell smoke and know I must leave. I find an exit and see a clear path out of the burning building. As I head down the hallway, I pass many people who are sitting and lying on the floor. They are aware of the danger, but for some reason they are unable to move. I look closely and realize that they have darker skin; they are Hispanic, possibly building maintenance workers. I hurry past them in my urgency to escape the fire, but pause just as I get to the exit door. I realize that I cannot let myself leave and must turn back to help them.

With little prodding, Karen could see the dream's message: success was betrayal of her community and ancestors. As irrational as it may sound, success as a prominent academic or manager was "joining the other side." For years Karen had fulfilled her family's dream of joining the mainstream, while maintaining a deeply Japanese devotion to her ancestors and to her community's traumatic World War II experience. The struggle of her immigrant people over seventy years had a deep hold on her, and it was keeping her at impasse.

Karen's situation was actually even more psychologically complex. As a woman and a minority in the world of engineering, and academic engineering in particular, she would often find herself in situations in which her contributions were undervalued. On the road to becoming an elite professional, Karen passed numerous reminders of how her family had been people at the margin. In her dream she was both the person with the power to be safe *and* the immobilized immigrant, powerless and vulnerable.

This dream allowed Karen to explore her deep ambivalence about success and joining the elite. She was able to reaffirm how important her career was to her. She was also able to reaffirm that her career was in the service of her family, her community, and the best wishes of her ancestors.

Karen remains to this day a champion of the underdog and has used her acute sense of organizational politics and power dynamics to help many students and fellow workers who have come to her for assistance. She sees this work as very much part of her vocation. She also recognizes that she need not stay in a burning building any longer; she sees clearly that self-immolation in paralysis and depression helps no one.

Demons

Both Raymond and Karen came from essentially supportive families who wished the best for them. That wish, at times, came with strings attached. In their cases, the strings were tied to a family system that demanded extraordinary achievement. The wish for a child to fill in the gaps in a parent's longing for fulfillment is often present: "I want you to experience what I was not able to." Although this wish may become an obstacle for the child, it springs from urges that are positive, perhaps even noble.

When parents' wishes are conscious and communicated explicitly, their children are less confused by agendas that may be at odds with the children's deepest instincts. The children can separate what is "theirs" and what is "their parents'" and can choose to accept or not accept their parents' perspectives. But sometimes such a desire is highly charged with the force of bitter disappointment or barely conscious resentment. Sometimes a parent cannot see a child as he or she actually is, and adjust expectations accordingly. When there is an unconscious and unspoken demand for the child to redeem in some way what a parent sees as his or her own life failure, then the work to break free is more complicated and is likely to take longer.

The ghosts (or actual presence) of parents who have strict agendas for their children can be real adversaries—and can be malignant and even dangerous forces in our attempts to move beyond impasse. Most cultures provide, in myths or stories, images that allow a child (or adult child) to understand what is going on when a parent's agenda overshadows a child's real needs for growth. The evil stepmother in "Cinderella," the witch in "Snow White," and the giant in "Jack and the Beanstalk" are classic examples from fairy tales of adult stand-ins for overbearing or antipathetic parents.

Popular culture, too, provides such images. In the movie *Dead Poets Society*, a father is desperate for his adolescent son, Neil Perry, to pursue one course and one course only in his life: a career in medicine. The father's desperation is such that, driven by disappointments or fears in his own life, he overlooks the personality, talents, and deepest desires of his only child, who wants to be an actor. Neil cannot bear to tell his dictatorial father that he has excelled as Puck in a prep school production of *A Midsummer*

Night's Dream. When the father threatens to pull Neil out of school and acting and threatens military school, the boy commits suicide.

It is a testimony to human resilience that most children are able to find their way to their own hearts even while under the burden of inappropriate parental agendas. We all have the capability to discover our passions. We do not have to change the past; we do not have to become a different person. We do not even have to solve the riddle of our family's complex dynamics. There is always a way to step forward, to gather in all that we can of what is most important in the time that we are given.

Releasing ourselves from the hold of the past is the project of a

DEEP DIVE

Stakeholders

During an impasse, when you are sitting by yourself and focusing on a big decision, you are never alone. Others are always in that room, others who have a point of view about the decision you are about to make. Raymond's older brother, and his father, are always in the room with him at such times. They unconsciously offer their views on what counts as achievement, on what is "good" and "bad" work. Karen's parents and grandparents, her uncles and aunts, and even her more distant ancestors, are in the room with her.

Who is in the room with you? Make a list of the stakeholders in a decision, whether in work or the wider reach of life, that you are facing or will soon face. What is the tone you hear when they speak to you? Is the tone loving, honest, and direct but with a definite point of view? Or, is the voice more of a whimper from the lifetime. Each step, built on an often modest insight into the nature of the hold as well as the will to break free, brings an opportunity to let something go.

In one sense, we can never fully free ourselves from the powerful presence of key figures from our youth. What we *can* do is raise our awareness and be honest about just how powerful their influence is. (See "Deep Dive: Stakeholders.") When we acknowledge that they are indeed "in the room," we begin the process of letting them have their say, and then discerning whether it does or does not agree with our own deeper and more authentic voice.

---

corner, a vague complaint about something that is hard to see or understand?

For each of these highly influential figures from your youth, answer the following questions:

- What was his life dream?

- In what way did he realize it?

- In what way did he fail (what is his "unfinished business" in life)?

- Who are her heroes? Whose career does she admire or envy the most?

- How does she see your strengths and weaknesses?

- What has been her message to you about what you should do with your career?

- What do you sense is important for her that she has never admitted directly?

> - How does he try to influence your decisions?
>
> - How does she show approval or disapproval?
>
> - Right now, do you think he is satisfied with the choices you have made?
>
> Write a brief portrait now of what you know about what each of your "stakeholders" wants for you, and for themselves, from your career and broader life. Then, when you hear that point of view being expressed in your own deliberations, you will know who is speaking and will be able to listen without either being immediately convinced or rejecting the suggestion out of hand.

One thing more: we must want to let go. Will must accompany insight. We must wish to be free; we must make the concerted effort to give up the familiar and open to a broader vision that denies us of the company of habit and personal history. We tend to cling to what we believe will give us some sense of belonging or comfort, even if the price we pay for the clinging is high. The woman with a history of childhood abuse finds herself in an abusive relationship. She may choose to stay because that relationship not only echoes the family of her past but also represents the greatest sense of connection she believes she can hope for. The businessperson puts off family and hobbies in pursuit of more wealth long after he has attained financial security because his role in his original family was that of the superachiever. Giving up the comforting chains of the familiar requires a glimpse of a larger and more spacious possibility. It also requires the willingness to let part of who we thought we were die. Only then can something new take its place.

The Shadow

Tom Wilson was forty-three years old when he first came to see me. A licensed clinical social worker, Tom had split the past fifteen years of his career between a community mental-health center and a private psychotherapy practice. For as long as he could remember, he was drawn to being a counselor.

Those who know him well would describe Tom as empathic, sensitive, and intellectual. The impasse that brought him to me had been building for several years. During the 1990s, his profession went through a dramatic transformation because of managed health care.

Tom resisted the changes that required him to dramatically limit the number of therapy sessions for each client and engage in extensive paperwork and was able to maintain a somewhat reduced practice working with those patients who were able to pay him out of pocket. He lowered his fees for those to whom this presented a hardship. Tom's real crisis, however, came at his "day job." His agency had been acquired by a larger organization and was undergoing a radical restructuring. There ensued a yearlong period characterized by daily uncertainty and high turnover. Staff jobs were being eliminated and new titles created. Several of his colleagues had already been forced out of their positions and had left the agency.

The churn at the agency served as a wake-up call. On one level, Tom had been in denial about the growing crisis brought by the advent of managed care. He enjoyed his private practice work in his book-lined office. He enjoyed being home when his preteen son returned from school. He enjoyed the ability to read poetry, his great passion, between clients and in the evenings. He had built a daily routine that seemed meaningful and agreeable, protected from the pressures of the corporate world in which many of his clients struggled. Tom had built a comfortable life for himself and his family.

Tom's first reaction to the changes at the agency and in the world of psychotherapy was to try to maintain the status quo. He imagined that he could preserve the nucleus of his private practice and, by keeping living expenses low, not have to compromise his satisfying lifestyle. But Tom was retreating from the challenge the recent changes offered. His denial was finally pierced when his own department at the agency was eliminated. This was when he came to see me.

Tom was filled with questions: Should he affiliate with a health maintenance organization? Should he market his private practice better? Should he apply for another job at the agency? Tom's first inclination was to move closer to what felt most comfortable. He considered leaving the agency altogether and focusing on his private practice but was concerned about his ability to pay his son's educational expenses. He saw his home office and his books as an island of refuge. Then a dream came.

> I am in my kitchen at home. I am wearing comfortable clothes and making pancakes for a group of guests. I come to realize that these guests are in fact an army. They are about to be deployed on a mission, to go out into battle. My job is to be the cook, and at some level I am relieved that I will get to stay behind.
>
> As I am working at the stove, an officer comes into the kitchen. He tells me that every man is needed for the battle and that I must leave right away to join the troops headed for the front. I know that I have no choice and that this is my destiny.

It would take many months for Tom to comprehend the message of this dream: that it was time to summon the energy of the warrior and do battle. Something larger in his life was demanding that he leave his domestic tranquility and turn his attention outward to the wider world. (See "Deep Dive: Selves Left Behind.") The idea of such change evoked fear, even as it presented opportunity.

Tom decided to seek a leadership role in a new unit that was emerging out of his agency's restructuring. This role would not be full time, but it would allow him to build, with a colleague, an "employee assistance program" that would provide basic initial counseling services for smaller businesses that could not afford the expense of larger, established programs. Tom and his partner could use their network of colleagues whose private practices had been reduced by the recent changes to supply these services.

DEEP DIVE

Selves Left Behind

Reading biography—even the brief passages above about Tom, Karen, and Raymond—inevitably generates associations relevant to our own lives. What have you left behind? What part of yourself gets left out?

Before you read further, take time to capture the associations, memories, and feelings that emerged as you read these stories. Do not worry about deep analysis. Just pay attention to the particular place you found your mind going as you read about Raymond, Karen, and Tom. The images may not seem related to those stories or even important, but write them down anyway. A brief paragraph or two will suffice; write more if more seems to come spontaneously.

Tom was surprised at the energy that seemed to emerge from nowhere once he made the decision to go forward. But right now, it would be sales and marketing skills, not counseling ability, that would make or break this business plan. Tom began to tap into a part of himself, the extroverted salesman, that he barely knew existed. He had always viewed himself as a compassionate listener, a dad, a lover of poetry. He could be tough when necessary, but aggressiveness was not a major feature of his self-image.

Impasse was telling the warrior to step forward.

The warrior was one part of Tom's "shadow," a figure that plays an important role in the psychology of Carl Jung. We all have the potential to live from the totality of our being, Jung believed—from all of the instincts, drives, and longings that make us human. As we are socialized, we assume roles in our families and in our wider social world that define a narrower version of our identity—our conscious ego. This ego gives us a particular place in the world, as the sensitive caretaker perhaps, or as the aggressive businesswoman. But these narrow roles come at a cost; other elements of our experience get tossed out in the sculpting of our particular identity from the totality of our full self. For Jung, growth happens when we recover disowned shadow elements of our being. The shadow is different for each of us, but impasse offers us an opportunity to learn more about energies that have always been there, but have not been included in our mental model of our own "self."[1]

Today, Tom manages a consortium of counselors who provide employee assistance to twelve small and medium-sized businesses in and around New Haven, Connecticut. He continues to enjoy his private practice, his books, and helping his son with his homework. But he also spends a lot of time planning business strategy with his partner and making sales calls. He entertains the thought of expanding the business to at least thirty clients. He is proud of his increased income and what it means in terms of possibilities for his family. No one in Tom's immediate family had ever been in business, and he now realizes that he had projected, in a critical fashion, much of his own ambition onto so-called corporate types. Half a lifetime of projection had resulted in denial of his own "warrior self." But now he relishes the renewed energy it brings.

For Tom, impasse meant a "return of the repressed." It often does. We all make compromises—"deals" that take place in an internalized world where the emotional stakes are high and the choices are often unconscious. Sometimes necessity drives these choices; bills indeed need to be paid. But many times they are driven by a self-image shackled by artificial notions of who we are and who we are not. Such a self-image is surely headed for impasse.

As a crisis deepens into impasse, there is a return of the repressed. Ancestors and demons come back to haunt, and the crisis may call on parts of ourselves that we have left behind. As these ghosts from the past surface, we feel completely stuck. It is all too easy to misinterpret this state as "failure." But impasse is not failure at all.

When a life crisis or impasse shakes things up, it weakens the defensive structures we have built up to repel aspects of being that, for whatever reason, we had unconsciously labeled as "not me." With these defenses weakened, we find ourselves with the opportunity to live a part of ourselves that had been left behind.

The Accuser

William Blake, the visionary English poet and artist, led a bold life of poverty for the sake of his art, but his work achieved little recognition in his lifetime. There was always a voice telling him that he was wasting his life, that his etchings and poems were useless, and he was a man who could barely support his family. The voice would grow loud precisely when he was about to throw himself into some new project that was full of promise but also of uncertainty and the possibility of failure. Blake excelled at naming psychological dynamics and personifying them so that he could deal with them as characters and make them recognizable. Sick of this persistent voice, Blake gave the speaker an identity so he could recognize it and wave away its attacks. He called it, after biblical tradition, the "Accuser."

The irrational, harsh critic whom we have internalized is today referred to by a variety of names, such as superego, inner critic, and bad parent. Freud may have coined the term superego, but the concept was immediately recognizable to his readers, for this brutally critical naysayer has been part of the human condition through the centuries. The primary meaning of the Hebrew word for Satan is *accuser*. Early Greek translations of Hebrew scripture maintained this meaning with the word *diabolos*, meaning "one who speaks against." The diabolic is, at its root, that which speaks against the human impulse to grow and experience life more fully.

The Accuser is the voice that tells us that we have failed, that we are inadequate, that we have made the wrong choices, that we are unworthy, or that we are not attractive enough. This Accuser says that our energy for innovation and our readiness for change are impulses not to be trusted. The superego is the hyperdeveloped brake system for human initiative. The psychologist Eugene Gendlin faults Freud for calling the superego "the conscience." The superego is *not* the conscience; it is not moral, it is not the "small, still voice" of the Bible. Rather it is "the loudest voice within us," and its concern is not to redress wrongs or take moral action; its concern is to punish and *stop* us from taking that action which would allow us to experience new possibilities.[2]

The inner critic can be crippling. We must learn to recognize this enemy, for recognition is the first step in preventing this adversary from stopping us. Each of us has an Accuser with a particular personality and a specific way of delivering a disheartening message. If we do not recognize the Accuser, then our feelings of guilt, shame, or inadequacy are vague and undifferentiated. They become merely "who we are" rather than the voice of an unhelpful intruder. (See "Deep Dive: Recognizing Your Accuser.")

DEEP DIVE

Recognizing Your Accuser

As you read about the internal critic, images of your own Accuser will come to you. Bring them on.

The "same old stuff" is different for each of us. Take the time, right now, to pay attention.

What comes as you focus on the phrase "the same old stuff"? The same old painful stuff. You should have . . . what? You are too . . . what? If only you could be more . . . what? You are too old now to . . . what?

When these lines come, pay attention to how they affect you. Where in your body do you feel them? Do your shoulders begin to slouch? Is there a tightness in your stomach? Do you get suddenly restless and get up to leave the room? Do you begin to daydream?

The first step in silencing the internal critic is knowing what the feeling is, what the experience is in the body, as well as the content of the accusing "message." Know that the Accuser is speaking and also that there are other voices in you, voices that speak with greater authority, and accuracy, about your reality and what the world offers.

The Accuser can manifest a self-critical presence in many ways, using many voices. For people who are at impasse, the Accuser is often part of the conversation. The two forms this intruder frequently takes are those of diminished self-confidence and deep-seated regret about choices made and opportunities missed. People in their twenties and thirties are more prone to a lack of self-confidence. People in their forties, fifties, and sixties are more susceptible to reproach themselves for insufficient accomplishment or to devalue the very real contributions they have made to their families, their communities, and their professions.

The Accuser can be a killer of the spirit, and is responsible for much of mid- and late-life depression. Lawrence Kohlberg, a professor at Harvard and the most recognized writer in the psychology field of moral development, talked in the months before his suicide of how much Freud and Jung had accomplished by his age, and how far short of such standards he and his colleagues had fallen. When the Accuser has free rein, it does not matter how many degrees we obtain, books we publish, deals we complete, or titles we achieve—it will know how to make us feel inadequate.

External forces can sometimes magnify the voice of the Accuser. Demand for accomplishment (as defined by the collective ideal) varies with national and regional cultures, but those of us who are American will be familiar with our culture's intense and unbounded demand for financial accomplishment and public recognition. It seems that the spirit of entrepreneurial individualism has a shadow side. The ideal of standing out and, paradoxically, being acknowledged for standing out, can contribute to the devaluation of accomplishments that do not register on the mainstream scoreboard. (The Dalai Lama has commented that he was shocked by the level of self-loathing he found among adults in the West.)

Accomplishments in relationships, in the development of families, in community building, in artistic expression, and in religious experience are often excluded from the "scoring system." The Accuser would be the first to agree that they simply do not count. Not *really*. (Why are music and art programs always the first things cut during school budget reviews? Why do parenting accomplishments, or leadership roles at church, synagogue, or mosque rarely show up on résumés?)

I have listened to many clients in their forties or fifties make the case to me that they are underaccomplished and have made either poor choices or insufficient effort. Rarely in this stinging summary will I hear mention unqualified inclusion of a successful marriage of twenty or more years, of the wonderful personalities of children nurtured, of a passion for mountaineering or mountain biking, of contributions to school committees, pastoral councils, or local arts associations. "No points," says the Accuser.

Disarming the Critic, Healing the Self

As crisis deepens into impasse, we might become so discouraged that we put our old defenses to work rather than sticking with the impasse until we are able to open up to a new type of information. Because the Accuser is almost always a guardian at the gates of impasse, we must all develop skillful means of dealing with it so that we can move on.

There are both immediate and long-term strategies. The first step is to know that the critic is not "us." Following Blake's lead, we must name this figure immediately when it steps into the room. The Accuser is here! It is beginning its predictable diatribes! Whether the Accuser is Dad, Aunt Edna, your meanest teacher, or a combination, give that inner critic a name. We need to know that that inner voice is *him* speaking, or *her*, and that what he has to say is, as Eugene Gendlin points out, inaccurate, distorted, simplistic, amoral, repetitive, and boring. It is the same old stuff, one more time: "I am not pretty, I should have gone to law school, I should be a vice president by now, I should have taken that job with Microsoft back in 1986, I should have married someone different."

Once you realize that the Accuser is present and doing his thing, there are some good moves to use in countering his attacks. Gendlin, in *Focusing-Oriented Psychotherapy*, lists five strategies to keep in mind. The first is "disrespecting the superego": to acquire this disrespect, notice how unreasonable, negative, stupid, and repetitious the superego is. The second strategy is "remembering to not believe the message": know how and where to find an accurate account of what happened—talk to your friends or colleagues who were actually present when the Accuser said you messed up so badly. Their account of the situation is likely to be quite different from his.

The third strategy is most relevant to the work that we do at impasse: "Go back to what was happening *just before* the superego attack." Clearly, something threatened the status quo. We were getting in touch with something exciting but threatening. Then the criticism started pouring in. What was it? Where were we? This going back shows us where the frontier of our impasse is. The critic often attacks just as we are about to take a new step forward. Going back shows us what the new step is, and gives us a chance to stare down the Accuser as we make the choice to move forward.

In his fourth strategy, Gendlin counsels us to merely "wave the superego off." Just say good-bye: Don't argue with, defend against, or verbally counter the superego. Say simply, "Yes, yes. I've heard all that. I don't need to listen to it again." It is even better to say nothing, just waving the hand to move the superego away. The last strategy? Use humor! If we can stand far enough back, this boring repetitive act becomes comical. Gendlin suggests rolling one's eyes: "Come back when you have something new to say."[3]

The Deepening

We often experience impasse as a sense of deflation and sinking to a lower place, whether it is brought on by a crisis at work, or by a sense of emptiness or "missing out." We all have experienced this cycling: from the mountaintop of confidence to the valley of inertia. Impasse is a low place, but it is also a grounded place. You may feel heavy, even weighted when you are there, but you are closer to the center of things that are important, closer to the fullness of being alive with its joy and its pain. This is a coming back to our "truer" selves, a coming back to our essence before the layering of expectations and family dynamics took hold, before we made compromises for survival. When we feel this sinking, which at first seems to offer only loss and disorientation, it is important to remember that we all have an instinct for the way out.

If we admit to ourselves that we are deep in the valley, and if we can refuse the Accuser's attempts to shame us for not being on the mountaintop, then new possibilities are available. We can open up, we can see that our old maps are no longer useful and let go of the plans that came from those maps. Now we are truly explorers, with an urgent desire to see the terrain ahead for what it actually is. We need to take a closer look at this business of throwing away our outdated maps.

THREE

Opening Up and Letting Go

T HE SENSITIVE YOUNG POET Rainer Maria Rilke lived much of his life "in his head," concerned with literature and philosophy. Wandering one day in the Louvre, he found himself captivated by a fifth century BC statue of Apollo. Only the torso remained, the head having been lost centuries earlier. Rilke realized that this god communicated his presence and energy, his "light," fully and directly with his body. No head was even necessary.

Standing in front of the statue, Rilke found himself becoming aware of a dimension of life he had been missing without even knowing it. "We cannot know his legendary head / with eyes like ripening fruit," Rilke wrote in the poem "Archaic Torso of Apollo," "And yet his torso is still infused with brilliance from inside, / like a lamp, in which his gaze, now turned low, / gleams in all its power."[1] The power, Rilke realized, was coming from Apollo's entire body, not from whatever thought or mood the face, had it existed, might have communicated. He ended the poem as follows: "Otherwise this stone . . . / Would not, from all the borders of itself, / burst like a star: for there is no place / that does not see you. You must change your life."

The message hit him hard: existence is not a cerebral affair; he would now need to approach life in a different way altogether. His former "mental model" of life could not explain his experience in front of the statue. "You must change your life," he concluded. Indeed, something was already changing.

Opening Up and Letting Go of Our Mental Model

We all have an explanation of the way things work, and of what makes us tick. Psychologists often use the term "mental model" or "cognitive map" to describe the inner roadmap we use, consciously or not, to find our way through each day and make decisions, big or small. A mental model can be seen as an accumulation of a lifetime's learning about what works and what doesn't. We have a model for our boss's personality and how she will respond to certain behaviors; a model for things that will go well for a family outing and things that won't; a model for how to get ahead at work; a model for how to navigate the local traffic flow to get to work on time.

The problem with any mental model is that it is always operating on information from the past. In contrast, true vision is never an arrangement or rearrangement of solutions that have worked in previous circumstances, but springs from the immediacy of today. We get a new boss, our children grow, our department at work is reorganized, road construction radically changes commuting patterns.

Life is always breaking our mental model. We are continually being surprised by events and by people who do not meet our expectations. After all these years, we thought we knew our spouse completely; then he does something that makes us realize his reality contains things we had not yet mapped. We read a book or have a conversation that, like Rilke in front of the statue, makes us realize that we have missed something vital all along. A life shock momentarily awakens something in us, and for a moment we are fully alive, with no model at all. We all want this, to be touched directly by life itself. So a crisis that thrusts us into the middle of things with no plan for escape allows us a chance to figure out what is really important.

When we release our conditioned and obsessive hold on our preconceptions, we are often surprised by the feelings, the imagery, and the energy that come rushing in. Mental models tamp a lot down, keeping information out of our awareness. What we need then is a means for temporarily suspending our mental model so we can let these feelings, images, and instincts drift up again. The first step is to find a way to break our conditioned habits of thinking so our attention is free to look deeper into our consciousness, toward information that is always there and available. In the remainder of this chapter we focus on a process for temporarily suspending our mental model of life and our place in it. In chapter 4 we learn more about taking the step that Rilke took in shifting his awareness to a new type of information.

Free Attention

Not all of us have the artistic sensibility of a Rilke, or the ability to find the perfect image in the world around us and use it as a departure point for an already well-nurtured, ripe imagination. But with perspective, we can all learn to let go of old models and open up to new ones.

A first step is to practice "free attention." Some mastery of this practice is necessary in order to take full advantage of the exercises that follow later, to engage an open concentration that is alert and yet not attached to the images that will emerge. Free attention is a freedom from distraction, an alert presence that requires an intensity of focus akin to that of a climber walking the knife edge of a mountain wall. It requires everything we can bring to it.

When practicing free attention, we are working against the powerful conditioning of our egos. By ego I mean that part of the self that wants to keep everything familiar by labeling and categorizing. Ego places new experiences that might pose a threat to the status quo into old boxes so we can judge them and react to them efficiently. Every day we wake up to this whirring and buzzing world and our ego starts to sort things out, making them seem familiar. Disruptions to this status quo are inherently threatening; if allowed to become conscious, they may evoke anxiety. It is ego's job to keep that fear, and what lies beneath it, at bay.

So in the face of a new day of experience, ego begins to make plans: we make decisions about how we are feeling, what clothes to put on, what to eat for breakfast, when we need to leave the house to get to work. We choose to seek out some people and avoid others. We listen to the news and form opinions so we have some sense of order and mastery over the information that continues to barrage us as the day progresses. Ego allows us to feel more safe and to be decisive, but at a cost. We may suppress new information that is at odds with the status quo. Ego interprets the world using shorthand, and in doing so it may miss important information.

Ego is likely to resist the practice of free attention. It does not want us to face the fear that whatever will come up will in some way be threatening, that we will not be able to "do it," that we will not be able to tap the energy and act on the instinct just beneath the surface.

However, when we are at an impasse, we need new information, especially information about what is *missing* rather than a summary of what is *already there*. The practice of free attention allows us to take in this new information. It does not eliminate ego, but rather suspends the judgments that prevent us from seeing and intuiting more deeply. It is this quality of alert, intense, and non-judgmental looking that Marcy Kaufman brought to the image of the red van and that Rilke brought to Apollo's torso.

Practicing free attention is the art of being more fully present. It is much more than just relaxing. It is simple, but not easy. That is why it is a practice. For starters, the practice involves setting aside ten or fifteen minutes any time we feel the need to "step back" and, at least temporarily, suspend the noise and the narrowness of our current mental model. We can use it as a preliminary approach to any creative task we face. It is also a practice that can serve as a prelude to the deeper imagination exercises in chapter 4. (See "Deep Dive: Practicing Free Attention.")

DEEP DIVE

Practicing Free Attention

You may wish to skip this section and return to it when you have time to work with it without interruption. As it is better for you to do the activity without having to read your way through it, have someone read this section to you. Better yet, let me guide you through it. Go to the Web site associated with this book (www .careerleader.com/gettingunstuck). If neither a friend nor the Internet is immediately available, read the directions in short chunks, getting the essence of each part of the directions before moving on.

Sitting in a chair, find a comfortable position with your feet flat on the floor. Allow your posture to be alert without straining, your spine straight, and your hands relaxed and resting in your lap. You are aware of sensations; some of them seem to be "inside" your body, others on your body's surface. Allow your attention to rest on sensation alone. You are aware of perceptions and thoughts that come spontaneously. Thoughts are followed by choice and judgment: something is good or bad, right or wrong; this exercise is interesting, intriguing; this exercise is strange, tedious. These judgments, too, come automatically.

As you sit, you are also aware of being conscious of this whole process unfolding. And this consciousness draws in associations, memories, images, and further thoughts and reactions to these mental perceptions that start the process cycling again.

Now, respond to this simple instruction: "Place your attention on the palm of your right hand." Do not look at your hand, do not clench your fist. Simply place your attention on the palm of your right hand. This free attention can be held, but it is not easy to do so. Even as you focus on your hand, the unending flow of perception, feeling, reaction, thought, and judgment continues. You have a thought and a reaction to that thought: Where is this going? What is the purpose of all this? Your attention is no longer on the palm of your right hand. You have lost your free attention.

Return your attention to the palm of your right hand. You are learning the work of holding free attention. You're practicing the craft of presence. Now shift your attention to your left kneecap. As you hold your free attention on your kneecap, notice the competition for your attention: you are reacting to these very instructions, you are thinking, evaluating the usefulness of the exercise or even of this book itself. Your feelings and thoughts compete for your open, unattached, attention.

Now, shift your attention to your breathing, but do not slow it down or speed it up. Simply allow your free attention to follow your breath naturally. Keep your attention focused on your breathing as you continue.

With your attention on your breathing, note again the competition for this attention. Perhaps you're already thinking about tonight's dinner; perhaps you're wondering if you should skip the exercise altogether. When you realize that your attention has been distracted, simply bring it back to following your natural breathing (or, if you are uncomfortable placing your attention on your breathing, focus on the palm of your hand). Notice that holding free attention in no way blocks the unfolding of your total experience. You experience the form of your body and forms around you and are aware of sensations and perceptions. All of this unfolds as your free attention remains with your breathing, witnessing the whole process without judgment.

Your awareness of perception continues. You have reactions and feelings, you have thoughts about these reactions and feelings, the thoughts continue to rise and fall way. At times, stronger feelings may arise. You may become aware, in your gut, of a heaviness that only later you are able to recognize as fear or sadness. Let it be there, let it do its work on you. Do not try to change it, do not try to avoid it. It is emotional evidence of your arrival at a frontier, an assurance that you have returned to a place that ego has retreated from before. Do not embellish, encourage, or discourage these feelings. Allow them to emerge and run their course. Keep your attention open. This frontier has its own shifting emotional weather, and you are open to whatever that weather brings.

Your awareness continues uninterrupted. Your attention stays with your breathing or on the palm of your hand. You are not an outside observer. This is presence: alert, watchful, and purposeful attention.

As you continue to sit, continue to bring your attention back to your breathing or to the palm of your hand. Note that your focus is not inward. You are not creating an image of your breath or your lungs; you are not "meditating." Your gaze is straight ahead, you are aware of your body, and this gaze, this awareness, is your presence. Your gaze itself is an extension of your attention; you can move it from a point immediately in front of your face to a point several feet directly ahead or even widen it to the boundaries of your peripheral vision. As you do this, your attention, although it remains focused on, merged with, the point of focus you have chosen, comes more and more to fill the space around you. Notice that the sensation of body does not have hard boundaries; your presence fills the entire field of your perception.

While you are practicing free attention, you may feel discomfort or tightness in your abdomen, solar plexus, chest, or throat. If this happens, you may wish to simply place your attention right there and patiently focus on that place. Pay attention to what images emerge when you do so, but do not cling to those images or attempt to analyze them. Allow them to emerge, form, and recede while you return your attention to the "border" of the physical sensation itself. If this becomes too uncomfortable, simply return your attention to your breathing or to the palm of your hand. If at any point these practices make you feel too uncomfortable, discontinue them for the time being. The border is always there, and you can return to it when you are ready.

The practice of free attention allows us to clear a space at the center of our awareness and see the many ways in which we are still hanging on to pictures or models of our life that are no longer accurate. As we get better at this practice, we become better able to see how the thoughts and tensions that arise during the exercise are really the very places where we are caught. It is here that we have anxieties and fears based on assumptions that have led to unrealistic expectations of ourselves or others. Here we still harbor disappointment and resentment that things haven't turned out the way we imagined they would last week, last year, or a decade ago.

The practice of free attention shows us how we let expectations and mental constructs get in the way of opening up to the way things actually are, right now. It is a useful practice on its own as a skillful means of identifying hang-ups and, to the extent that we are able, letting go. It is the work of a lifetime to become good at this, but work that we can benefit from right away, if we make the effort. As we gain proficiency, we move more directly to the place where we can feel our "holding on" and then practice the act of letting go of our attachment at that stuck point.

This practice of free attention is an end in itself. Doing it is an essential movement toward becoming "unstuck." It is also a preparation for the next step in the vision and impasse cycle. By clearing a space, we prepare ourselves for being able to recognize what is pushing in our lives to fill that cleared space. When we have let go enough to listen well, we can begin to ask the question: What is really important, right now? What new information do we need to pay attention to? Is an action required? Once we have relaxed the grip on our mental model, a new effort is required. From the vantage point of the cleared space of free attention, we must now open up to a new type of information.

FOUR

Shifting to a New Understanding

CHRISTINE DUPREE was twenty-eight years old and a second-year student at the Harvard Business School when I first met her. She is someone who injects warmth and intensity into any conversation, but even more so when talking about her twin passions: the arts and community service organizations.

"Music was important to me from an early age," she told me in our first meeting. "What I wanted to do when I grew up was to both sing and teach voice. I went to a performing-arts high school half a day as well as a college-prep high school half a day, and performed on the side.

"It is also important to know that I grew up in the church," she continued. "My father is a Methodist minister and a professor of the

New Testament, and my mom is a professor of education. So I came from an academic background and a community-focused background. Being involved in the church, I did a lot of volunteering with homeless shelters and adolescent programs at the local community center. In high school, I apprenticed to a chorus program for inner city youth and got to perform in schools and got to teach some of the kids."

Like most students coming to business school, Chris did not have a preconceived destination. She did not come from a business family nor did she major in economics or business in college. She had done well at the entry-level jobs she took right after college. She knew that business graduate school would open up many possibilities, but she was not sure what path she should follow. As she looked around, it seemed that many of her classmates were beginning to focus on their career goals (most of them were, like her, still at sea with this process). With the energy generated by hundreds of fellow classmates focused on their career direction struggle, just being in graduate school was creating an impasse. The clock was ticking; graduation seemed uncomfortably close. What was really important for her? How should she focus her efforts?

Through an impasse life is saying, "You are not paying enough attention to vitally important themes and tensions. Stop now and identify them." Moving through impasse to a new place requires both the letting go that we worked on in the free attention exercise and the opening up to a new type of information that can move us forward.

Making the Shift

This shift to a new type of information comes when we have "come to the end of our thinking" (that is to say, from the end of the thinking that is possible using our old mental model). The shift can occur in many ways and can be catalyzed by different means. Much of Carl Jung's work was devoted to helping his psychotherapy patients recognize the messages of the unconscious mind, through a greater awareness of the images that come from dreams, art, and techniques such as his "active imagination."[1] In many approaches to meditation, the practitioner is guided through a process that allows a shift away from the information and associations of the discursive mind to information and knowledge available from more intuitive and sensing-based modes of apprehension. There are many stories of dramatic shifts that people experience when faced with a sudden danger that forces them to call on capabilities and instincts they barely knew they possessed.

We can cultivate the ability to shift to a new perspective and a new mode of understanding. The Vietnamese Zen teacher Thich Nhat Hanh tells the story of a difficult decision he faced during the Vietnam war. Nhat Hanh was the leader of a community imperiled by the growing conflict in their immediate area. How could community members protect themselves? To whom could they appeal for help? Should they go or stay? Nhat Hanh turned these questions over and over in his mind to no avail. He got up and began to do a meditative "walking practice" that he had cultivated for years as part of his Zen training. He walked slowly in circumscribed patterns, doing the specific practice that goes with this method. After many hours, the answer became clear to him. They must leave right away. Leaving one's home and becoming a refugee is never an easy decision, but in this case it was necessary. In retrospect, this decision, difficult as it was, saved the community.

Analytically breaking down and examining each piece of information that was available to his discursive intellect hadn't helped

Thich Nhat Hanh. The various alternatives each had their pros and cons, and a great deal of information was simply missing. However, by shifting to a deeper and more intuitive mode of understanding, he was able to grasp the whole of the situation, and when the decision came, he knew at once that it was right.

Again and again life demands that we let go of the surface features of analytical thought and move closer to the core of our being and our being-in-the-situation. Rarely will the demand be as urgent as the one Thich Nhat Hanh faced, but each demand requires that we arrive at a new type of information before we can move forward.

In my work with students and clients I have developed several exercises designed to enable a shift to accessing a new type of in-

DEEP DIVE

The One Hundred Jobs Exercise

Step One: Select Your Most Exciting Work Roles

Reading through this list of one hundred occupational roles, select the twelve roles you instinctively feel would be the most exciting, engaging, and meaningful. Move rapidly through the list and use your first intuitive impression. Do *not* consider whether you have the skill or training to perform well in that role. Do *not* consider its financial rewards. Identify the twelve roles that would simply be most engaging.

When you have selected your top twelve, rank them with number one being the work role you find most exciting. If your

formation or, more accurately speaking, to a new focus. These exercises are not infallible techniques—they work only if we feel the urgency and make the effort. But that effort is rewarded when we focus our attention on the themes, images, and dynamic tensions that carry essential information we had overlooked when performing analyses based on outmoded mental models. To help Christine Dupree move along the incipient path to her future, I led her through the One Hundred Jobs exercise. This exercise is a deceptively simple procedure for identifying essential work and life themes. Before we learn from Chris's experience with this exercise, each of us should do it on our own. (See "Deep Dive: The One Hundred Jobs Exercise.")

first choice is much more important than your second, you might leave an inch of space on the page to indicate this. If your first and second choices are essentially equal in importance, list them one after the other with no space in between.

One Hundred Jobs Exercise
List of Occupations

1. Marketing researcher
2. Child-care worker
3. Computer software designer
4. Sports coach
5. Manager at a manufacturing plant
6. Salesperson in a retail store
7. Social services professional
8. Salesperson for high-tech products
9. Litigator (courtroom lawyer)
10. Psychotherapist
11. Manager of a retail store
12. Public relations professional

13. Advertising executive
14. TV talk show host
15. Theologian
16. Speech therapist
17. Newscaster
18. Secretary
19. Automobile mechanic
20. Electrician
21. Entertainer (singer, comedian, etc.)
22. Optometrist
23. Professional actor
24. Senior hospital manager
25. Fine artist
26. School superintendent
27. Leader of a product-development team
28. Religious counselor
29. Financial analyst
30. TV or film director
31. Personal financial advisor
32. Director of human resources
33. Graphic designer
34. Economist
35. Business strategy consultant
36. Homemaker
37. Senior military leader
38. Chief executive officer
39. Librarian
40. Research and development manager
41. Real estate developer
42. Music composer
43. Veterinarian
44. Advertising copywriter
45. Senior manager of a manufacturing business
46. Nurse
47. Ship captain
48. Research sociologist
49. Manager of information systems
50. Investigative reporter
51. Medical researcher
52. Chief financial officer
53. Office manager
54. Police officer
55. Investment banker
56. Manager of a restaurant
57. Entrepreneur
58. Vacation resort manager
59. Electrical engineer
60. High school teacher
61. Professor of political science
62. Theoretical physicist
63. Computer systems analyst
64. Fiction writer
65. Newspaper editor

66. University professor
67. Military serviceperson
68. Diplomat
69. Venture capitalist
70. Military strategist
71. Logistical planner
72. City planner
73. Accountant
74. Bank manager
75. Architect
76. Carpenter
77. Manufacturing process engineer
78. Firefighter
79. Marketing brand manager
80. Surgeon
81. Investment manager
82. Stockbroker
83. Director of nonprofit organization
84. Event planner
85. Administrative assistant
86. Credit manager
87. Elected public official
88. Motivational speaker
89. Mayor of a city or town
90. President of a community charity
91. Real estate salesperson
92. Professional athlete
93. Clerical worker
94. Foreign trade negotiator
95. Bookkeeper
96. Emergency medical technician
97. Statistician
98. Manager of a stock or bond mutual fund
99. Proofreader
100. Civil engineer

Step Two: Identify Underlying Themes

Looking over your list, identify themes that seem to tie together many of your occupational role choices. A theme does not have to apply for all of the choices on your list, but it probably should be present in at least four or five of them. Examples of themes are:

- Love of technology
- Finance

- Creativity

- Managing

- Power and control

- Influence

- Structure

- Entrepreneurship

- Tangible products

- Teamwork

- Energy and passion

- Public service

- Autonomy

- Interpersonal transaction

- Doing rather than analyzing

- Individual contributor

- Customer contact

- "Front room" rather than "back room"

- In the spotlight

- Intellectual challenge and problem solving

- Helping people

There are innumerable possibilities. The goal is not to get as many themes as possible but rather to find the wording that truly captures each essential element that underlies your list. Be creative. Push yourself. The first few themes come easily, but the most useful and least conscious are likely to come at the end of your theme analysis just when you are most tired and ready to quit.

Step Three: Identify Dynamic Tensions

Dynamic tension is present when a theme seems to apply to several occupations on your list, while other occupations seem to contradict that theme. An example of such a tension might be "Maximum Financial Gain vs. Public Service" or "Autonomy vs. Leading Teams." Some people's lists contain a number of dynamic tensions, others' contain none. We all have such dynamic tensions in our personalities and in the visions of our lives. One part of the self finds attraction in one direction and another part of the self is drawn to an apparently contradictory direction. Working with these tensions is a necessary part of growth. Your job now is to simply identify any tensions you can.

Step Four: Paying Attention to Spontaneous Images

As you work to identify themes and dynamic tensions, continue holding your free attention. You will from time to time become aware of images that come to you spontaneously. These images may also come later when you are rereading your list and the new list of themes and dynamic tensions. Examples of images are "standing in a spotlight," "walking a tightrope," "standing on top of a mountain." Images may also come in the form of popular songs that occur to you as you do the exercise. Write every image down, as irrational or irrelevant as it may seem.

You will end up with a written document containing your list, as well as themes, dynamic tensions, and images that emerged from your work on the list. This is a living document that you can return to in the future when you do the exercise again, or when other exercises stimulate deeper imagination. The real product of the exercise is an expanded understanding of the themes that are essential for you at this time in both work and life.

The Shift:
Working with a New Type of Information

Once we have generated our list of themes, images, and dynamic tensions, we must amplify and analyze them so that we can understand them and their message as fully as possible. To help us with this process, I interviewed Chris after she had done an extensive analysis of her One Hundred Jobs experience with her "career team." (At Harvard Business School, students work on career impasse in small groups called Career Teams.) The theme analysis of the One Hundred Jobs exercise can be even more powerful when done in a small group. Each person takes a turn in the spotlight and the other members of the group generate his or her themes, images, and dynamic tensions. The person whose list is being analyzed simply records the group members' comments. At the end, he or she can join the analysis and ask the other members to expand on their comments. Steps three and four can also become more powerful in a group setting. Doing the exercise in a small-group setting will provide a wider range of images, themes, and dynamic tensions. When working with a small group it is helpful to use a large "flipchart" so that all group members can view the original list and the emerging lists of themes, tensions, and images as the work proceeds.

This is what Chris had written as her top twelve choices, in rank order (Chris was using an earlier version of this exercise, so the wording of some of her choices is different from the wording used in the exercise in this book):

1. Music director (changed from TV or film director)

2. Director of a social service agency

3. Elected member of a congress or parliament

4. Research and development manager

(Chris left some space at this point to indicate that the choices above represented her "top tier.")

5. Entertainer (singer, musician)

6. Management consultant

(Again, another space to separate this grouping from the one below)

7. City planner

8. Architect

9. Leader of a product-development team

10. Research sociologist

11. Newspaper editor

12. Mayor of a city or town

Reflect on Chris's choices and write down the images that come to mind and the themes you recognize. What major themes emerge that would underlie many of these otherwise disparate choices? The most challenging analysis is the recognition of dynamic tensions— what themes seem to be contradictory? Chris's team identified nine themes, an unusually high number (four to five themes is the average range). Three particular images came to different members of the group during the exercise. Three dynamic tensions surfaced among the team members and an important fourth dynamic tension emerged when Chris had a counseling session with me after the group had ended.

Chris's team looked at her choices of music director, entertainer, architect, and city planner and saw a Creativity theme. They saw a Public Service theme in her selections of director of a social service agency, elected member of a congress or parliament, and mayor of a city or town. Looking at the number of selections that had a "manager" or "director" title or were elected public officials, Chris's team saw a Control theme.

Chris and I both agreed that the team's Community theme was a big part of her life story reflected in her volunteer work and her high level of involvement with extracurricular groups at business school. I asked her next about the Diversity theme: What did her team mean by "diversity" and what does that mean to Chris?

"It means two things," she answered. "The first is diversity of interests; being in jobs where you're doing different things, playing in different worlds, talking to different people. But diversity, I've come to discover, also means the type of people you get to deal with, which ties into the Business vs. Artist dynamic tension. Finally, because I grew up in Atlanta, cultural and ethnic diversity are enormously important to me."

"How about the Energy and Passion theme?" I asked.

"That's what drives anything, and anyone who's successful has to love what they do," she replied. "When I took a job as an internal auditor after college and juxtaposed that against my work with the community chorus, I decided I was just cheating myself because I wasn't doing something I was passionate about. And I found that having other people around me who are passionate is just as critical."

"So that's an element of organizational culture, being with other people who are excited about what they are doing, that you're going to be looking for?"

"Yes, definitely," she said.

I encouraged her to explore the Tangible theme.

"It to me doesn't mean that I need to be able to see that a widget comes out the other side to be happy. In fact, I'm sometimes more comfortable working in the theoretical world than in the truly pragmatic. But it comes back to seeing something happening. Purely theoretical without any result, just to have thought the thought, isn't a very efficient use of anyone's power and creativity. I loved singing but it was even more fun to direct the community chorus and to see a program through from conception and rehearsal to performance. To see the power of it and its impact on people."

Chris was less loquacious when I asked her about the Structure theme. She at first didn't even think structure made a theme. I prodded, and she offered her thoughts:

"I think about it more as sort of that problem-solving approach than I do the type of environment that I would be working in. Although I guess when I think about all the jobs that are on my list, there's an element of structure. Like with a performance there's a timeline."

"How about the Needing Teams theme?"

"I think that's very, very true. When you're dealing with something that's creative and something that's out of the box and new, teams are really important. No one person has all of the brilliant ideas. I find the team dynamic exciting. Everything I look at now has to have some sort of team element."

Then I shifted to a discussion of the dynamic tensions her team recognized. They had called the first one Doing vs. Observing.

"I definitely feel that tension," Chris mused. "I think that's the tension that I see as academic vs. pragmatist. If you put my twelve jobs into either an arts bucket or a business bucket, you see that tension in both buckets. You'll see entertainer being the person on stage and you'll see music director, the person who's making it happen. Within the business bucket you see management consultant but also leader of a product-development team. I think a lot of people have that tension of 'I want to advise people, tell them how to do it and I want to be the one to do it.' It's definitely a challenge finding roles that have both."

"The 'two buckets' you mention reflect the Artist vs. Analyst dynamic tension your team identified," I responded. "Also, your team saw you as someone who enjoys problem solving on your own and who also enjoys a leadership role. They called that dynamic tension Individual Contributor vs. Leader or Manager."

"I think that one's probably the least clear to me simply because I'm not quite sure where I fall. I love team concepts and I'm very happy to step back and just be one person. At the same time when I see a problem, I see solutions, and if I don't feel like things are going that way, then I want to be the leader."

Finally, we looked at the three specific images different members of Chris's team experienced while working on her material. They were: "kissing babies," "onstage in the spotlight," and "cutting the ribbon."

Christine laughed. "I think I was uncomfortable with all three of those images. It's funny. I don't really want to be a senator, but I like the concept of what they do. I think my team hooked onto that. It's an interesting theme because the first two images come from my two biggest passions, different as they are. Kissing babies definitely ties into the public service image, and the next one, being in the spotlight, into the arts image. But because I still love the conceptual work, I usually don't think of myself as being the person getting the reward and the spotlight, but at the other times I do. I constantly mull over in my mind whether that spotlight image needs to be kept in check, but I don't know if that's the right way to approach it."

I found this interesting. It struck me as a dynamic tension that Chris's group did not recognize, "Serving Others vs. Being the Star." "The way you were pushing it away makes me want to probe it more," I said, "because this is something you're not fully owning. And I think you are being judgmental about the 'Star' pole of the tension. This is something for you to look at. Martin Luther King, Jr., would not have been able to serve unless he had been able to take the spotlight when it was very dangerous for someone with his background to do so. I think you can find many examples like that. Is this a frontier for you?"

"Yes, I think so. Part of it's a tension because of the value judgment, part of it's a tension because I'm just a strong introvert, and so there's an element of the spotlight that sounds exhausting to me. I'll need recuperation time to recover from that constant out-there personality. But at the same time, when I look at the jobs that I want, I value being able to stand in the spotlight. So while I don't want to think of myself as someone who needs attention to feel rewarded, I think it's interesting to think about—can I use the attraction to the spotlight as a tool rather than as a distraction?"

"There is real energy and genuine meaning here for you," I replied. "And, for some reason, you're uncomfortable with it. It is something that you tend to label 'not me.' 'Being in the spotlight' wants to come out and find itself in your daily life."

The Shift: New and Familiar

The "shift" is a "dropping down" into more imaginative and less conditioned ways of looking at ourselves and our world. Every venture into exercises such as the One Hundred Jobs is a return to our essence, as it is speaking to us at the present moment. We shift from cognitive analysis based on an old mental model to information that comes from giving our essence a chance to speak in the fresh language of image and metaphor. This "new view" may indeed have a very familiar feel, for it comes from the core of our being. Rilke was able to recognize the message of the Apollo statue because his life of instinct was always there, waiting to emerge and take its rightful place in his daily living. He always had a life of the body with its instinctual intelligence, but his mental model of what was important had been blocking that intelligence for many years. The experience with the image of the statue allowed him to wake up and own what was already in place. Chris's need to express power and put herself forward as a recognized leader was not new, she had simply not acknowledged and allowed for how important it really is. "All knowledge is remembering" Plato observed.[2] The shift is a deeper kind of thinking that allows us to find words for things that have been important all along. (See "Deep Dive: Further Work with the One Hundred Jobs Exercise.")

DEEP DIVE

Further Work with the One Hundred Jobs Exercise

The One Hundred Jobs exercise resulted in a list of the key themes, dynamic tensions, and images that came to you spontaneously. From reading about Christine's experience with this exercise, you can get a sense of how these can reveal a new type of information about essential life themes. Return to your own list. Can you expand on the themes and tensions you identified? Do new images come to mind as you reread your list?

Although the One Hundred Jobs exercise is based on stimuli from work roles, it is not just a career exercise—the themes that emerge are relevant to both work and life.

Deepening the Shift

Amy Orlansky called me two years after she had attended an executive education class I had taught in San Francisco. Then fifty-one, Amy had led a rich and varied life. With undergraduate degrees in philosophy and computer science and an MBA from the Kellogg Business School, she had worked in her early twenties in a successful rock band and later in a strategy consulting firm and a *Fortune* 100 corporation before moving to San Francisco to start a family. When she was in her forties, she and her husband and their two young children had lived in a remote African village as part of a church mission. At the time of the workshop, Amy had been living in San Francisco for many years, and, partnered with her husband, operated a real estate business from their three-bedroom flat.

Amy has always oriented herself to the needs of others, and when she came to the workshop, the demands on her attention were many. With a daughter in high school and a son, several years younger, who was learning disabled, Amy's responsibilities as a parent were substantial. That, combined with her business partnership with her husband, left her little time to herself. Her very decision to attend the workshop was, at some level, the beginning of an awareness that change was necessary.

When Amy called two years later, she was eager to work with me in career counseling. She reminded me what she had written in response to an exercise I had led two years earlier.

> I see a wood-paneled room, like my office. I see light and windows and plants. I don't feel other people. I don't feel what it is that I am working on. Instead, it is a peaceful, confident feeling.

Somewhere I feel creative people or a team near me. Am I a writer? An artist? I am not accountable to a client, am I? I am just there, at peace in a warm, indoor garden. I don't want to work? Just be?

I do see art, I don't see the struggle, and I see the beauty, the result the unity of peace and confidence, light and green, and warm wood. Authenticity.

I am alone, it seems, and this is worrying me as I become conscious of what I am writing . . . I am in charge, in control, using my mind.

The exercise that had prompted Amy's vision is one I call Image Gathering. I developed it after many years of working with clients who were at impasse, when I realized that most were starting in the wrong place in their attempts to move forward. They were either trying to "think through" their situation or they were immobilized by the overwhelming emotions of the impasse. There was no way for a new perspective to find its way past the barrier of either old ideas or a fear of drowning in feelings of depression, anxiety, anger, or shame.

Cultivating Images

Clients at impasse who come to see me all share one thing: they are feeling stuck, and the next right step is not clear. Months or years earlier they may have been deeply engaged in the work they were doing or deeply satisfied with their lives. But for some reason they now find themselves unable to focus. After a few hours of conversation, this often begins to change. Almost always this "stuck" person is able to offer all sorts of information about who he is, and about how he is different from everyone else around him. He is able to call up memories and images about those times when work and life have deeply engaged him, and what those memories and images mean as far as the new situation that, at some level, he knows that he now wants.

So if this information is there, why can't we just reach in and pull it out? The Image Gathering exercise is designed to get us back to the place where we can tap those impressions of what it means to be fully engaged in a way that is fully satisfying.

It shouldn't be so hard to sense such information, but somehow it is. There is a clear "signal" down there sending messages about who we are and how we're different and what that means about finding satisfying work. But for most of us, noise jams that signal.

As we saw in chapter 2, conscious and unconscious messages from important people in our lives often barrage us. Messages from our culture about what work is good, what work is prestigious, and what success means also assail us. Messages about what a good life is add to the noise. Our fears about our lack of knowledge or skill, or just about life generally, add to the cacophony.

How do we silence the noise and home in on the clear signal about who we are and what work we were born to do? How do we formulate a vision of a newer, truer life? What we do *not* do is begin with analysis. A new life vision has to come from employing all aspects of our consciousness to realize a full-bodied experience of the self and the situation. It has to arise from deep intuition.

Image Gathering is an exercise that summons this deep intuition. There are two versions of this exercise; one is focused specifically on career vision, and the other on broader life vision. You may participate in either or both of these exercises by letting me lead you through them at www.careerleader.com/gettingunstuck. This exercise, unlike the One Hundred Jobs exercise, is not necessary in order to use this book fully. It will, however, add to the variety and texture of the insights you gain from the One Hundred Jobs exercise.

In the Gathering Images exercise, we start by letting images come to us through a guided meditation. Just images. What do we know in the depths of our being about the work environment we want, the types of people we want to have around us, the types of activity that will engage us every day? Like a vivid dream that grips us even after we awake, an image taps all aspects of awareness and may include visual, emotional, and intuitive dimensions. These sensing, feeling, and intuitive dimensions can be complemented by a "thinking" or analytical awareness as well.

The Gathering Images exercise moves through three phases.

- The first phase circumvents our day-to-day conditioned thinking and elicits the essential images associated with a new, emerging vision.

- The second phase, a writing phase, highlights these images for closer inspection. This writing is the start of a living document that we may return to as often as we need to continue envisioning our future path.

- The third phase analyzes the deep imagination brought on by the first two phases. It involves a specific approach toward this disciplined imagination.

We must learn how to let the images work on us before we can begin the work of appreciating the coded messages they bear. The images that arise from the Image Gathering exercises lead us to look at aspects of ourselves and our world that are not "in the future" but are already there, awaiting discovery.

These images are preverbal messages, aspects of self-aware-ness that have not yet been processed through the language cen-ters of the brain. In being preverbal they have a premonitory quality. They bring news: hints about what might be if we are able to get the message and act on it. They point to knowledge about ourselves and our world that will be known more completely only later, when we have had time to take it in fully and express it in words.

Once we have collected these images, we will go back and say, "So what are the patterns here?" Then we will bring our analytical consciousness to bear and say, "What are the core themes? What are the dynamic tensions?" Analysis can help us become strategic and tactical about how to move forward. First, though, we must slow down.

Amy's Images

Amy had been surprised by what had come to her during her first Image Gathering exercise. Here are Amy's responses to the seven questions I asked at the end of the exercise (I would add two more questions two years later):

1. What is the essence of two or three core activities that showed up in your images?

    Alone, at peace, clear concentration

    Using my mind, writing

    Creative team nearby

2. List five adjectives that describe the atmosphere of where you were in your images:

    Clear, concentrated

Light, happy

Nature, green, wood, light

Peaceful, creative

Alone but not lonely

3. List five more adjectives that describe the people around
    you in your images:

    Separate, independent

    Creative, synergistic

    Subordinate or equals (but not boss or authority)

    Friendly team

    Cooperative, helpful

4. Who does this type of work (the work that showed up in
    your images during the exercise)?

    Marjorie (sculptor)

    Writers

5. Who else does this work?

    Joyce (sister, small design firm)

    Painters

    Julie McArthur, author

6. When in your life have you been closest to the work that
    showed up in your images?

    PR project for not-for-profit organization

    Writing book about rock band experience

    Making the photo project

7. When in your life have you been farthest away from the
    work that showed up in your images?

    Working for consulting firm (office atmosphere)

    Working for a money center bank

    Sharing an office with Martha

    Working with Victor (PR) in his office

    Working in my ugly subbasement studio

When Amy called me two years after that executive education
class, she wanted to move to a deeper analysis of these images. In the
intervening months, she had begun to imagine being a marketing, public relations, and general business consultant to artists and nonprofit
organizations, something that she had recently done quite success-
fully for a San Francisco sculptor. We scheduled a counseling session.
In that session, I asked her to respond to the two new questions:

8. What's going to stop you from realizing the vision indicated
    by your images?

    *Continuing to let the family business dominate my
    time*

    *Always taking care of people: children, parents, and
    sisters*

    Fear

    Inertia

    *Feeling that I should continue to be available for
    family (daughter in trouble, son with special needs,
    husband used to my help for last twenty years, father
    dying and needing help)*

Fear that my age (fifty-three) is going to stop any group from taking my application seriously

Embarrassment that my résumé reads like an adventure story, that I will be seen as a dilettante when what people need are specific talents

Fear that although I have a good sense of strategy, it is all based on gut, and I need further training to call myself a business consultant

Inability or unwillingness to carve out time to discipline myself to work through these barriers

A feeling that there is something missing in me, fear of exposure

No office, no private phone, and no uninterrupted free time: i.e., fear that to do a search well or even to accept clients or a project, I will be overwhelmed by trying to do it in my present environment—yet am I ready to rent an office and fly solo?

9. Who or what will be your strongest allies in making your vision real?

Strong inner compass

"Spiritual" daily practices that ground me

My own strengths: humor, vision, creative energy, and true sense of adventure

Strong inner belief that this is my path—that I should not stay "hidden" and safe

At the time of the original exercise, Amy had been surprised that the most compelling image placed her in a large room—and there were no other people there. She found this very troubling. "Perhaps," I had said then, "what you need now in your life is more space." In fact, after the workshop Amy became drawn to Buddhist meditation, working with a teacher versed in the Tibetan tradition. The practice of visualizing and meditating in open space as an experience of free, unconditioned, and unbounded existence became the foundation of her spiritual work. Finding "space" had indeed been what this busy mother and manager of a family real estate business needed most.

There was nothing prophetic in what I had said. I was looking at her image and reading it in the same way I would approach any image in art, literature, or dream. The image was a message from a preverbal aspect of awareness that was pushing for full expression in Amy's life. It was there because there was a real urgency in the message, an urgency that moved Amy to begin to imagine what she needed next. She acted on this sense by starting her Tibetan Buddhist practice.

Amy's story suggests how we can take the images that come to us through the Image Gathering exercise and apply them in life. The application need not be something as esoteric as beginning to practice Tibetan meditation. The message might well be that what you need is more money, or a schedule that leaves more time for family or for going to the theater.

Understanding the Images

After we finish with imagining and writing, we can begin the next phase of our vision work: decoding the images that surface. The first step in decoding is to simply pay attention to the way the image is affecting us. For Marcy Kaufman, it took careful attention, bringing a charged awareness to bear, before she could truly understand the image of the cherry-red van. Packed into this one image was the emotional "meaning" of her father's presence in her life: strength, warmth, protection, caring, and presence when he was needed.

Like Marcy, Amy at first had little idea what the image of an empty room with no other people meant. She was shocked, for her previous understanding of empty rooms was "loneliness" or "alienation." Only by paying attention—studying an image with the full being (thinking, feeling, intuition, and sensual awareness)—was she able to experience the message of a need for more space and realize that meditation would get her into that special room.

We too must pay attention to images, which is an art in itself. If you are an appreciator of painting, sculpture, or poetry you have already had some initiation into this art. As you spend more time not analyzing, but simply paying attention to how images affect you, your skills in this art will grow.

Once we have identified an image, our first tendency is likely to be to assign it to categories, theories, experiences, or frameworks we already know. If we do this, we will miss the new message. We need to enlarge the image, "amplify" it and let it grow inside of us until we see more of it, and in greater detail. We must learn to let the image lead and watch intently to see where it takes us, what it does to us. A theme may begin as an abstraction but amplification can prompt specific ideas for the way it needs to enter our lives. As we let the metaphors, images, and themes soak in, we will begin to notice what entertaining them brings to mind, and how they affect us in a deep and very physical way. Letting an image work in your body is a way of "knowing with your bones."

When life forces us to make difficult choices, having an idea, as insightful and intelligent as it might be, is not enough. We must act from the deepest place possible, understanding and assenting with the very fiber of our being. Soon we become accustomed to making decisions from that place. It moves us beyond what is sentimental or dreamy. It is a practice for returning to what is most important, to something deeper than our wishes, opinions, and flights of fancy. It allows us to return to our core.

The Themes Behind the Images

Once we have settled on a suite of images and learned to know them in our bones, we can proceed to a more analytical process of understanding them. Looking for themes involves coming up with general principles based on the raw data of the imagination experience. Themes capture the "deeper" message latent within the specific images.

As a way of beginning, refer back to Amy's images earlier in this chapter. Look at all of imagery: What are the essential elements that would best capture the essence of all of this information?

Here are the themes that Amy and her workshop colleagues found in her spontaneous writing, in her answers to the questions, and in imagery that surfaced as we reviewed them in our later counseling session:

Creative work so important

Solitude status quo but meeting with others at my discretion

Important to integrate work into entire being, comes from inside

Really important: CONTROL OVER ENVIRONMENT

Create environment that is nourishing, refreshing, what the spirit needs to be at peace, to spark the creativity

Working on my own terms without judgment or pressures

Doing something unique, creative in peaceful, harmonious place

Picked up teaching element—intense potential to help others not to feel bogged down by "noise"

Helping people see that other things are important (beauty, serenity)

In these themes we see the need for her own space, for more creative work, for control over her time, for the ability to make her own work decisions, for both a sense of solitude and connection with creative collaborators, and for altruistic service.

Amy found a way to move beyond just creating a sense of personal space through meditation; eventually this sense of space began to express itself as assertive independence and she was able to bring this experience into the way she worked with clients. Working with this new more expansive sense of herself, as well as with her vision of a deeply personal way of working as a consultant, she expanded her business to serve small companies in the areas of marketing, business systems, and negotiations. The idea of personal space could now be put together with her desire to engage the world outside of her family more actively. She began a new cycle of "giving" that drew on deeper sense of her own work rather than on the demands of her husband's business.

The analytical challenge for both the One Hundred Jobs and Image Gathering exercises is to extract the deep metaphors, themes, and dynamic tensions that underlie our choices (from the One Hundred Jobs exercise) and our images (from the Image Gathering exercise). The imaginative analysis is what completes the shift to a way of understanding our situation that is at once refreshingly new and familiar.

Amy was able to act on the new imagination of her situation that came from the work that started in her workshop with the Image Gathering exercise. She was helped by the fact that she had many experiences and deep self-awareness to draw on. The self-awareness we gain from each episode of this impasse work accumulates over time. With this growing insight, we gain a greater understanding of the life patterns that hold meaning for us. Understanding those patterns is the task we take up next.

PART II

Vision

T. S. Eliot once said he hoped that if a critic looked at all the poems he had written over a lifetime, the critic would be able to see the "pattern in the carpet." Eliot imagined that individual poems—from whatever inspiration and written on whatever topic— would ultimately contain enduring, and repeating, threads. The pattern these threads formed, Eliot hoped, would reveal the themes that were most important for him, each finding its way into his artistic expression, and into his life, in different ways at different times.

Each of us has a "pattern in the carpet." Certain recurring themes signal what is vital for us. From these themes we can discern the types of activities, work environments, and close relationships that make our lives most satisfying. As we grow, we more easily see these patterns and make better choices for ourselves. Vision is not a one-time event; it builds over a lifetime.

FIVE

Our Deepest Interests

The First Pattern in the Carpet

I N EARLY JULY OF 2005, Lance Armstrong was headed for the most demanding stretch of the Tour de France in his quest for an unprecedented seventh championship. He faced mile upon mile of gear shifting and leg pumping, higher and higher into the thin air of the Alps. No stopping.

Feats like these have made Armstrong an icon to many people around the world, the model of a person who has aligned his life with his deepest passion. Armstrong started competing in triathlon events at thirteen and turned pro at sixteen. But when he was diagnosed with cancer at twenty-five, even his racing sponsor doubted his ability to recover and dropped him from the roster. Quietly, with extraordinary determination, Armstrong responded to his life-threatening illness not by retreating and changing course, but by redoubling his commitment to his sport. With a new sponsor, he returned to racing in 1998 and began the succession of victories that would place him among the greatest cyclists of all time.

Many of us share Lance Armstrong's passion and intense focus, even if we don't make it to the front page of the *New York Times*. Champion carpenters and champion surgeons and champion elementary school teachers are working at this moment, offering a combination of expertise won through years of effort and flashes of intuitive insight. But how did they come to their genius? How can any of us know that *this* is it, that *this* is the thing to which we will give everything we can?

To be sure, mining talent and developing skill is part of the story. But there is something deeper at work. We don't leap out of bed in the morning because we are good at something. We leap when we are excited. This excitement is a sign that, at this time in our life at least, we have found our place in the world. But how do we find our true place? And once we find it, how do we stick with it? After all, the world doesn't always cooperate: fame, money, prestige, and status tempt us; envy, debt, fear, and the turbulence of life place obstacles in our paths.

Armstrong won his race, excelling as usual in the grueling uphill stages. His victory was a tribute to what can be accomplished when we commit to a calling that engages the deepest levels of our being. It is possible to develop an ever-sharper vision of such callings, at work and in life, by looking for the significant patterns that emerge from our One Hundred Jobs and Image Gathering exercises. From them, we can develop talismans of identity, reliable reminders of where to look when we face inevitable changes in our life circumstances.

Lifelong Passions

For a very few of us, lifelong passions are explicit from a very early age (Tiger Woods hitting golf balls in his father's garage at age three, for example). For most of us, though, they remain latent through childhood and adolescence. The deeply intuitive parent may have insight into a child's deepest enthusiasms. But children and adolescents have not yet spent enough time in this world to test for themselves which places, things, people, and activities are truly the most meaningful for them.

This story changes as young adults enter their early twenties. Life interests start to show themselves with more consistency than they did during adolescence. As young adults grow older and learn more about the interaction between themselves and the world, they know themselves better and have a greater capacity for making choices that feed them in deep ways.

Research that has been done on lifelong interests reveals that these interests are among the most stable features of human personality.[1] By "interests" we do not refer to a love of tennis or a penchant for Italian opera. We refer, instead, to underlying basic elements of human interest and the way we rank one or more of these basic elements over the others. Mature adults have particular patterns of lifelong passions that remain stable over long periods. I refer to these basic lifelong passions as deeply embedded life interests.

Insight into the pattern of our deeply embedded life interests allows us to better predict the activities, work environments, living circumstances, and types of people that we will find most fulfilling. Those interests are among the most important "patterns of meaning" to consider when asking the question, "What are the enduring features of my personality that I should bear in mind when making major decisions?"

For many years, I have studied how deeply embedded life interests express themselves in life settings. I have been particularly interested in the way they manifest in organizations, where most of us spend most of our working lives. In collaboration with Dr. James Waldroop, my colleague on many research projects, I have developed a model in which deeply embedded life interests can be translated into what we call the basic "business core functions" (we use "business" here to refer to the broad context of organizations: for profit (both manufacturing and service), not-for-profit, government, even the military). These core functions telegraph the way different personalities find meaning in different types of activities. They help us better understand the challenges most important for us at work or in our broader lives (and they are relevant whether or not you work in business).

The Ten Basic Interests

By analyzing large databases of psychological testing, Waldroop and I have identified eight essential building blocks of all work that goes on in business organizations. In this book, I have added two dimensions from the work of psychologist and career theorist John Holland, so that our model encompasses virtually all work-related, deeply embedded interests.[2]

The eight "business core interests" identified in my research, along with two dimensions from the research of John Holland, constitute what I will refer to as the Ten Basic Interests. These ten interest dimensions comprise a system that allows us to analyze and rank our most important life interests. Most of us have significant interests in more than one of the ten dimensions; some of us even have significant interests in four or more. For the purpose of pattern recognition, all can begin by identifying their top two or three "personal highs."

First, let us review each of the ten dimensions of deeply embedded life interests. Each of the ten has a shorthand title ("The Engineer," say, or "The Artist") in addition to a research label in order to make it more memorable (see table 5-1). For each of the dimensions, there will be list of the job choices from the One Hundred Jobs exercise that are most closely associated with that particular dimension. It is important to realize that these "job choices" are not employment recommendations, but rather metaphorical images to help us identify our most important life interests.

The Engineer:
An Interest in Application of Technology

The Application of Technology function represents interests often associated with engineering: fascination with technology, systems and processes, and how things work. People with this as a "personal high" core function are interested in the "black box" aspects of life: How does this really work? How could we make it work better, more efficiently? Where is technology going and how could it be applied in my life? In organizations, people with a dominant interest in this area will enjoy roles in production and systems planning, product design, computer programming, operations process analysis, systems analysis, research and development management, and the use of technology to accomplish organizational objectives.

If this is a "personal high," we are curious about finding better ways to use technology to solve problems. Over time we will probably become comfortable with the "languages" of technology: mathematical analysis, computer programming, or various representations of the world founded on scientific models. Outside of work, we bring

TABLE 5-1

Recognizing the pattern

The ten basic interests

Deeply embedded life interest	Essence	Themes and images
Application of Technology	An engineering-like approach to problem solving; a love of technology and how things work	Expertise, innovation, problem solving, planning, engineering, science, gadgets, cutting edge, technology
Quantitative Analysis	An approach to understanding the world through mathematical analysis	Finance, analysis, control, math, investments, expertise, forecasting, modeling, precision, deals
Theory Development and Conceptual Thinking	Abstract and imaginative theorizing and analysis	Learning, problem solving, teaching, research, knowledge, ideas, debate, imagination, theory
Creative Production	"Blank page" creativity	Brainstorming, creating, new projects, designing new products, fast pace, free thinking, making art, loving ideas
Counseling and Mentoring	Emphasizing relationships and interpersonal concerns	Relationships, altruism, social enterprise, making a difference, teaching, counseling, psychology, people
Managing People and Relationships	Team leadership	Teams, leader, manager, mentor, goals, vision, motivation, people
Enterprise Control	Strategic decision making; control of entire operations	Strategy, vision, leadership, control, ownership, power, decision maker, player, principal
Influence Through Language and Ideas	Desire to influence and persuade	Ideas, knowledge, persuasion, writing, speeches, communication, power of language, influence, presentation, deals
Hands-on Problem Solving	Action; pragmatic problem solving	Action, service, craft, skill, strength, sports, tangible results, tools
Ordering Information	Creation of order and routine	Order, routine, predictability, certainty, detail, structure, care

an engineer's eye, and an engineer's enthusiasm, to projects that require careful analysis and planning. We enjoy gadgets and keep pace with the latest consumer technology. We find meaning as active participants in the ongoing technological transformation of world culture. Our hobbies are likely to be related to technology or science. We care likely to be the one to whom family and friends turn to with technical problems, say when a new computer application must be installed.

We likely have this core function as a personal high if the One Hundred Jobs exercise led us to certain work roles: computer-software designer, leader of a product-development team, research and development manager, medical researcher, electrical engineer, logistical planner, manufacturing process engineer, civil engineer, manager of information systems, and computer systems analyst.

The Number Cruncher:
An Interest in Quantitative Analysis

The Quantitative Analysis core function represents an interest in solving problems through mathematical analyses. If this is one of our two or three highest core functions, we are most drawn to the "numbers side" of work—what the balance sheet reveals, whether the assumptions built into the business plan or sales forecasts are accurate, how the spreadsheet reflects market analysis. We are attracted to work where high-quality quantitative analysis lies at the heart of the organization's success. Outside of work, we engage in problem solving that requires mathematical skill. We are drawn to investment and money management. We are likely to be the one to whom family and friends turn for advice on financial matters.

This function often surfaces in concert with the two other functions most directly concerned with intellectual curiosity and methodical problem solving. When it is paired with Application of Technology, there is often a "working with things" flavor to our interests, and we enjoy work directly involved with product design or production, or with problems that emerge in operations-intensive environments. When the function is paired with the Theory Development and Conceptual Thinking core function, we typically love "working with ideas."

Work roles from the One Hundred Jobs exercise most closely associated with the Number Cruncher are: manager of information systems, financial analyst, personal financial advisor, economist, chief financial officer, investment banker, accountant, investment manager, stockbroker, credit manager, statistician, theoretical physicist, manager of a stock or bond mutual fund, and logistical planner.

The Professor:
An Interest in Theory Development
and Conceptual Thinking

The Theory Development and Conceptual Thinking core function involves problem solving at the conceptual level. If this is one of our highest core functions, we must have a steady supply of intellectual challenges to feel fully engaged at work and at home. Activities attractive to such people are research, economic theory, developing models that explain competition within a given industry, analyzing the competitive position of a business within a market, designing a new product-development or product-distribution process, and all teaching based on theory and imaginative thinking. Outside of work, learning and reading in science, the arts, politics, culture, economics, and human behavior give great satisfaction. If this describes us, we need intellectual stimulation to grow and feel fully alive. We may have histories of being labeled "eggheads" or "bookworms." We seek out friends who are also intellectually curious and always up for a discussion of international politics or the latest scientific controversy. Our socializing is likely to include a book club or membership in a group organized around an intellectual area of interest, such as foreign relations or environmental policy.

People with strong interest in both this function and the Quantitative Analysis function love the analytical nature of problem solving. Those drawn to this function as well as the Creative Production function engage in imaginative, visionary, and theoretical thinking.

Jobs from the One Hundred Jobs exercise associated with the Professor core function include: theologian, economist, business strategy consultant, research and development manager, research sociologist, medical researcher, professor of political science, theoretical physicist, and military strategist.

The Artist:
An Interest in Creative Production

People with high scores in this function often see themselves, and are usually seen by others, as "creatives." (The Creative Production core function is often correlated to the Influence Through Language and Ideas function, but the two are distinct: While the Creative Production function underlies creative pursuits in general, the Influence Through Language and Ideas function represents the creative use of *language* to influence and persuade.)

The Creative Production core function represents "blank-page" creativity. If we have a high score on this dimension, we love the "dreaming up" work projects. We are not afraid of ambiguity or the lack of models from which to work. The challenge of "nothing being there yet" is the point. We see an unmet need and ask, "What product or service would address this problem? Is there a business opportunity here?" Or, when someone shows us an idea, we imagine the most effective way it could be packaged. Outside of work, we find fulfillment in the arts, creative projects at home, travel, and taking new classes. Our friends probably see us as prone to a certain restlessness; we want to be involved in something "new" whenever possible. Activities or lifestyles that are routine will be difficult; we will seek ways to break out of "steady states." Our friends might call on us to consult on an interior decorating project or to help plan the itinerary of a special vacation.

In the business realm, this core function is tapped through creative activities such as writing a new business plan, new product design, the development of marketing concepts, the development of advertising ideas, the generation of new business ideas, the development of innovative approaches to business service delivery, event planning, entrepreneurship, corporate training and organizational development, marketing, marketing management, and public relations. It also includes working in the fine and applied arts: imagining a fashionable line of clothing, conceiving a movie, or designing a medical testing device.

It is not uncommon for people with this core interest to be ambivalent about entering the field of business per se. In counseling interviews, many business professionals who have a high need for creativity talk about having considered careers in journalism, creative writing, art, fashion, or architecture. Some have wanted to be inventors or entrepreneurs. During school they often have difficulty deciding on internships and focusing on post-graduation employment. These people are *not* inherently indecisive, but they are wary of being trapped in routine.

An added challenge is that work opportunities allowing for expression of the Artist core function can be ephemeral. Launching a new project may be creative but can become routine over time. Thus, the job that *was* a good match becomes less and less satisfying. (My experience suggests that Artists change jobs more frequently than average during the course of their careers. Their search for creative opportunity pushes them on. Those of us who thrive on such creative challenge need to realize that this employment pattern may be a consequence of our innate interest structure, and not necessarily a problem with perseverance.)

The jobs from the One Hundred Jobs exercise most associated with the Artist core function include: advertising executive, TV talk show host, singer, comedian, professional actor, fine artist, film director, graphic designer, musical composer, advertising copywriter, investigative reporter, fiction writer, editor of a newspaper, and architect.

The Coach:
An Interest in Counseling and Mentoring

The Counseling and Mentoring core function places great importance on relationships, in and out of work. If you ask someone with a strong interest in this core function to talk about what has been rewarding, he or she immediately begins talking about collegiality. These people find meaning in relationships with colleagues, customers, team members, and friends at work. Outside of work, friendships provide major life satisfaction. If this is one of our personal highs, we are likely to be the one who friends seek out to talk over a difficult personal issue. We are likely to volunteer for tutoring and mentoring roles. There is a high probability that we will seek to contribute to our communities through involvement in public service agencies and initiatives devoted to community building. Volunteer work or jobs in nonprofit organizations will be important activities. All roles, whether at work or in our broader lives, that involve coaching, training, and mentoring will tap into this core function.

If this describes us, management roles that offer the opportunity to work with other people and develop their potential will often be attractive. Because human psychology fascinates those with high

Counseling and Mentoring interests, the day-to-day work of an "in the trenches" line manager can be a natural fit. (Not every skilled manager who enjoys helping subordinates, clients, and peers will have a high score on this function, but those who include Counseling and Mentoring as a personal high will be managers who focus on people.)

Organizational culture and mission will be important to those who have a high interest in Counseling and Mentoring; they will be strongly attracted to organizations that value the development of workers and reward managers who focus energy on personnel development.

If Counseling and Mentoring is a strong core function for us, we will likely have altruistic motivations and may look for vocational or avocational opportunities that allow us to make a meaningful social contribution. If we place this core function as one of our most important, we will probably focus on the social value of an organization's products or services.

The definition of social value may differ from person to person, so high interest in this area does not mandate work in the stereotypical "helping" professions, such as education or health care. High Counseling and Mentoring individuals thrive in every industry and may work for highly profitable companies; they draw satisfaction from the fact that the company's products or services make real contributions to society or add value to consumers' lives.

The work roles from the One Hundred Jobs exercise associated with The Coach include: sports coach, social services professional, psychotherapist, speech therapist, school superintendent, religious counselor, nurse, director of human resources, high school teacher, director of nonprofit organization, child-care worker, and emergency medical technician.

The Team Leader:
An Interest in Managing People and Relationships

The Managing People and Relationships core function represents interests realized through working directly with groups of people as a manager, director, or supervisor. Those of us who have a high level of interest in this function enjoy the team management aspect of leadership positions. We deal energetically with interpersonal issues on a daily basis, and derive work satisfaction from relationships at the office. We like leading the team.

If Managing People and Relationships is a personal high, we will be interested in hiring, evaluating people for positions, motivating individuals, building teams, using compensation to achieve objectives, and getting the most from each individual and team. In contrast to the Counseling and Mentoring function, in which the primary focus is on the person, this function focuses on the goal, and managing people effectively is a means to achieve that goal. If this describes us, outside of work we will gravitate toward team leadership roles in family and community settings. We will enjoy being the one who gets a project organized and completed. We will relish roles such as PTA committee chairperson or director of the Friends of the Library. Given a modicum of interest in sports, we will gravitate toward coaching. We will likely be the one who steps up to (and enjoys) the task of working out the logistics for the family reunion or the big anniversary dinner. Not having the Team Leader as one of our personal highs does not mean we lack ability as a manager. The interests of many successful managers lie in other core functions less concerned with the interpersonal aspects of work. We may enjoy aspects of leadership related to strategy, politics, or technology.

Work roles from the One Hundred Jobs exercise most closely associated with the Team Leader include sports coach, manager at a manufacturing plant, manager of a retail store, senior hospital manager, director of human resources, senior manager of a manufacturing business, manager of information systems, office manager, restaurant manager, vacation resort manager, bank manager, director of nonprofit organization, and school superintendent.

The Boss:
An Interest in Enterprise Control

Enterprise Control describes an interest in decision-making authority for complete operations. Those of us who have high interest in Enterprise Control want to control resources to realize an organizational vision. We enjoy "running the show," regardless of what that show is. Whether or not we enjoy managing people, we like making decisions that determine the direction taken by a work team, a business unit, a company division, or an entire organization.

Outside of work, we want to be known as leaders in our communities and in cultural institutions. We will enjoy being the one setting the agenda, whether it is the daily activities on the family vacation or the mission statement for a community group. We want to be on the board of directors or, better yet, chairs, of important institutions and relish a role in determining the vision for these organizations. Whereas the high Managing People and Relationships person may want to coach the soccer team, a high Enterprise Control person would want to be the chair of the school board who initiates an entirely new community athletics program. Those who have personal highs in both of these functions will want to be the visionary *and* the person who leads a team through execution.

An "enterprise" can be a business, big or small, that has been or will be in existence for many years. It can also be a "virtual enterprise" that is here today and gone a month or two from now. Deals and discrete transactions such as sales, financial service transactions, and consulting projects count as "enterprises." Just as salespeople may prefer short or long "selling cycles" (how long it takes to clinch the sale from start to finish), Enterprise Controllers may want a long "cycle" for their enterprise (the life of a GE or DuPont) or a short "cycle" (a Wall Street deal that may take only a few months to complete).

People with a very high interest in Enterprise Control often need to be cautioned. They want to run something, but it may take years to ascend to CEO or general manager of a company. The Enterprise Control person may find it difficult to tolerate early career stages of learning and proving themselves capable of being at the top. Many such people get derailed early on, because they aren't sufficiently patient; for every phenomenally successful person who attributes success to impatience, many more have failed. The caveat "Don't let your ambition get in the way of your success" is an important one for Enterprise Controllers.

The work roles from the One Hundred Jobs exercise most closely associated with The Boss are: chief executive officer, chief financial officer, senior hospital manager, school superintendent, business strategy consultant, senior military leader, senior manager of a manufacturing business, ship captain, investment banker, marketing brand manager, elected public official, mayor of a city or town, and president of a community charity.

The Persuader:
An Interest in Influence Through
Language and Ideas

Persuaders influence through the skillful use of language. If this core function is one of our two or three personal highs, we believe the process of achieving a specific goal (getting someone to buy something, landing a contribution of time or money, earning a vote, snagging a new employee, attaining "buy in" to an idea) is as important as the goal itself. Some of us who have a strong interest in Influence Through Language and Ideas prefer oral communication, others written; some prefer one-to-one conversation, others delivering speeches to large audiences; some plan long campaigns to influence people; others prefer discrete interactions.

Negotiations, deal making, public relations, and the design of campaigns are examples of activities that realize such interests. If we have a strong interest in this function we thrive in environments that call for frequent interpersonal transactions. We enjoy ideas and probably see ourselves as having strong communications skills. We will want to be "at the boundary" of a work team, a business unit, or of an organization, where we will be in continual interaction with people from other teams or business units, or with customers.

Outside of work, if this core function is one of our personal highs, we become spokespeople and thought leaders. We follow politics and community affairs. When this interest is paired with an interest in the Enterprise Control core function, we may want to run for public office or hold political appointments that influence in the community. Expression of our ideas in the public arena will be important, and we may write either editorials for the local paper or book-length works of fiction. We probably enjoyed debate in school, and being persuasive in a lively conversation may still be an important source of satisfaction for us. The limelight is attractive, whether it as at the family dinner table, the meeting of the town council, or joining in a heated conversation over the headlines while waiting on line at the supermarket.

Work roles from the One Hundred Jobs exercise most closely

associated with The Persuader include: salesperson in a retail store, salesperson for high-tech products, courtroom lawyer, public relations professional, advertising executive, TV talk show host, newscaster, film director, advertising copywriter, investigative reporter, newspaper editor, diplomat, elected public official, motivational speaker, mayor of a city or town, and foreign trade negotiator.

The Action Hero:
An Interest in Hands-on Problem Solving

Hands-on Problem Solving indicates an interest in work roles that include action, adventure, and physical activity.[3] If this is one of our personal highs, we like practical problems to solve. We like outdoor activities and work involving tools and equipment. We probably admire the craft aspect of challenging work and strive to be seen as an accomplished master in our craft area, whether it is fine antique restoration, detailed carpentry, or dental surgery.

Outside of work we are likely to enjoy sports and adventure. Physical challenge, demanding craftsmanship, and problem solving around the home give us a sense of accomplishment, and we may become skilled amateur carpenters, mountain climbers, sculptors, or gardeners. Outdoor activities will likely bring pleasure and reduce stress. We may be perfectionists who pay exquisite attention to detail, whether it is in the intricate design of new bathroom tiling, the subtle spice combination in a new dish at our favorite restaurant, or the minimal scar left by our surgical procedure.

The work roles from the One Hundred Jobs exercise associated with the Action Hero include: sports coach, ship captain, police officer, carpenter, firefighter, professional athlete, electrician, military serviceperson, automobile mechanic, emergency medical technician, surgeon, and civil engineer.

The Organizer:
An Interest in Ordering Information

The Ordering Information interest is associated with work involving organizing and managing information and attention to detail.[4] If we have a "personal high" in this function, we are attracted to roles that require high levels of administrative acumen when the administrative task is managing information. Whether it is planning large events, managing the schedules of a busy professional office, or doing the complex work of a medical coder, we will thrive when the challenge is to bring order, structure, and clarity in situations that demand the processing of large amounts of data and the ability to manage time.

Outside of work, we will enjoy a well-ordered environment and take pleasure in creating a comfortable home. We will be the person to whom others turn to manage the details of special events; we know where things are and how to keep things running smoothly. We will prefer activities that offer a predictable routine and hobbies that give structure to leisure time.

The work roles from the One Hundred Jobs exercise most closely associated with the Organizer theme include: salesperson in a retail store, medical records technician, accountant, secretary, credit manager, clerical worker, proofreader, and bookkeeper.

It is important to realize that the Ten Basic Interests represent life interests and not just work interests. (See "Deep Dive: Your Personal Passions.") They are really personality dimensions and carry meaning for the types of activities and living environments that are important to us, in all aspects of life. These are patterns that prevail, whether we are in impasse or not, and will find different modes of expression at different times in our lives. Throughout our lives, these deeply embedded life interests will remain wellsprings of meaning.

DEEP DIVE

Your Personal Passions

Which two or three of the Ten Basic Interests are most important to you? You can use the results from your work with the One Hundred Jobs and Image Gathering exercises to help you answer this. Here is the scoring process:

1. Turn to appendix C. In the column on the left-hand side of the table find each of top twelve jobs you chose in the One Hundred Jobs exercise.

2. For each job, score one point for each of the basic interest dimensions listed for it in the right-hand column.

3. Finally, add up the points scored for each of the ten basic interest dimensions and note the two or three dimensions for which you have scored the most points.

If you have selected four or more of the work roles associated with a particular core function, it is highly likely that that basic interest represents an important theme for you. Be sure to do the actual counting. The value of the assessment is that it provides a quantifiable method for helping you see through blind spots you may have when you use your intuition alone.

In answering the first question after completing your Image Gathering exercise, you indicated two "core activities" that were most often represented in the images that came to you during that exercise. Translate your description of these "core activities" into the language of the basic interest mode. Use table 5-1 for help.

Once you have a good sense of your two personal highs, reread the sections in this chapter that describe those areas that represent the most important sources of your work and life passions.

SIX

Learning to Let Our Passions Guide Us

J OHN WU didn't fit anyone's stereotype of a Harvard Business School student. He was, for starters, a Baptist minister and, at thirty, had spent his entire career in nonprofit organizations. Even so, John had a clear agenda for what friends saw as his unpredictable decision to come to business school. Steeped in Jungian psychology, John had come to Harvard to explore and develop his "shadow" side—aspects of his self that he had been denying in his life choices.

And just what did he see as "shadow" material? Money seemed to be at the heart of it. John told me that there never was much money in his family, which had moved to Chicago from Taiwan when John was sixteen. His father had never had a job that paid a professional wage, and John himself had never been motivated to pursue a lucrative career. As an undergraduate, John was attracted to the humanities, and his faith had attuned him to the needs of his fellow immigrants and to those he saw marginalized in contemporary American culture.

After a decade of involvement in various ministries, John had become concerned that he was avoiding something. Was he afraid of marketplace competition? Was he cutting himself off from the mainstream of a culture where wealth was seen as a means for accomplishing both personal and altruistic ends? Were the "best and the brightest" to be found not in church ministries but in the dynamic offices of the leading investment banking firms? What was he missing?

"I think I would like to see what it feels like," John told me soon after he arrived at Harvard, "to earn a professional services salary."

John relished his time at the business school. He jumped in with both feet and performed well in his courses. He became student government leader and developed a strong circle of friends. His extraverted and compassionate personality enhanced the campus community. And, as his graduate-school experience moved toward completion, he got that hoped-for offer from a top strategy consulting firm. He left school feeling excited, filled both with a sense of accomplishment and with anticipation of the things to come.

A year and a half later John called and brought me up to date on his life. "Well," he said, "I guess I really am a minister after all." John worked as a strategy consultant for about one year, but the role did not suit him. His work seemed too abstract; he did not feel that he was making a meaningful contribution. He moved to Los Angeles, where he and a partner had started a thriving career- and life-coaching practice. He was also working with high-level government officials to launch a leadership-development program for young Taiwanese men and women.

"I enjoyed many of my colleagues at the consulting firm," John told me, "but it took me a while to realize that I didn't really share their passions. We seemed to be looking for different things, both at the office and in our lives. The work was interesting enough," he continued, "but something was missing."

John said he kept asking himself, "Why am I doing this? Where is it leading?" And he added, "I didn't enjoy the analysis as much as working with the clients, talking about their problems."

What pleased me most about this conversation was John's laughter. He clearly was not viewing his adventure into the heady world of strategy consulting as a failure—or as a waste of time. In the end, John took from the experience exactly what he was looking for. He had explored a part of the world, and a part of himself, that had been both foreign and compelling. He had answered an important question about his place among his peers in the mainstream of global business. He now knew that he could run with that group, he could do the work, he could "compete." He also knew that it was not for him. In his core, he was "a minister after all."

None of this surprised me. John's test scores on Counseling and Mentoring and Influence Through Language and Ideas (measured by a psychological inventory I have developed from my research), were high, with Counseling and Mentoring being exceptionally high. John loved one-on-one counseling, and he loved taking the stage in front of audiences eager to learn what he had to offer. Purely analytical work left him feeling cut off from the pulse of, what for him, was the "real" world.

There is no one who has not, at times, doubted that they are in the "right" place, doing the "right" thing. We all come to crossroads when our best insight seems worn, or just too abstract to be of use. The sheer uncertainty of the immediate circumstances overwhelms the insights we have accumulated. It is at these crossroads that we need to drop everything and listen for that "small, still voice within" that reminds us of what is important—in an ancient way, amidst everything that is new. The "solution" we come up with, what we actually end up doing, may be different every time, even as it flows from enduring patterns of interest.

Mining One Hundred Jobs for Clues

Sebastian Lee worked for many years in the human resources department of a large national consumer products company. During a period of impasse, he realized that he felt stifled in that position. He needed more challenge and a greater sense of urgency. And he needed to be his own boss. Sebastian joined one of my workshops and completed the One Hundred Jobs exercise.

By the end of the exercise, he had a list of jobs that resonated with what he knew about himself (Sebastian was using an earlier version of this exercise; his choices included some jobs that differ from the wording in the version in this book):

1. Entrepreneur

2. Management consultant

3. Psychotherapist

4. Mayor of a city or town

5. Fiction writer

6. Writer of self-help books

7. Real estate developer

8. CEO

9. Mediation and arbitration professional

10. Public relations professional

11. President, chamber of commerce

12. Elected public official

From this list, Sebastian and I extracted information about his deeply embedded life interests. The choices CEO, entrepreneur, management consultant, mayor of a city, chamber of commerce president, and elected public official, indicated that Sebastian's first personal high is Enterprise Control. Five other work roles (fiction writer, writer of self-help books, public relations professional, chamber of commerce president, elected public official) suggested Influence Through Language and Ideas as his second personal high. These two are actually of similar strength (a ratio of 6 to 5). This made sense for Sebastian as his role as a human resources professional required a great deal of communication and persuasion.

Sebastian's profile pointed to a leadership style that emphasizes communication and influence. Individuals with this profile are often highly skilled communicators and networkers. They thrive in environments such as sales, deal-oriented finance, and senior management and flourish in organizations where interpersonal influence and verbal persuasion are essential for success. In early career stages, people with this profile do well seeking out roles that require building networks, alliances, and business relationships. In later career stages, this profile is a positive match for both "inspirational leadership" at or near the top of organizations or in high-profile "rainmaker" roles in professional service firms or sales leadership positions.

Sebastian ultimately chose to open his own executive search firm, which was an excellent fit for someone with personal highs on Enterprise Control (The Boss) and Influence Through Language and Ideas (The Persuader). As an Enterprise Controller, it also made sense that Sebastian would feel comfortable as an entrepreneur.

As we see from the experiences of both John Wu and Sebastian Lee, the more we move toward the anchors of meaning represented by deeply embedded interests, the more we will find ourselves in work activities and environments that call on our deepest enthusiasms. If we know the signature of our deeply embedded life interests, we will be better able to see through the glitter and find the true gold in the opportunities that come our way.

Dynamic Tensions

I first met Lucinda Torres as we both stood in the wings of an amphitheater classroom at the Haas School of Business at the University of California, Berkeley. She was in her late twenties, with short auburn hair and an earnest and direct manner. She greeted me with a firm handshake, as one might greet another business professional at an initial introduction. Lucinda had just graduated from business school and was still unemployed. She had volunteered to participate in a live counseling session with me in front of a roomful of career counselors-in-training.

Anyone would be anxious under such circumstances, but in Lucinda's eyes I noticed a deeper sense of unease. "You know," she said, "I don't think my testing results are accurate. I know what I want, and it's not what those results seemed to suggest." She was presenting herself to me, the visiting lecturer, with poise and confidence, but the impression she gave was of someone summoning all of her resources and putting on a brave face. Here she was, not only unemployed in difficult times, but also about to bear her problems to a person whom she had just met in front of a classroom of strangers from around the country. I admired her immediately. I liked her genuineness and her spunk.

I hoped that a session in front of a counseling class would help Lucinda catch a glimpse of some of the patterns that were essential for her if she was to find her way toward exciting work. Before we sat down in front of the audience, I had noticed that Lucinda's highest scores were, like John Wu's, on Counseling and Mentoring and Influence Through Language and Ideas. These are the two basic interests most associated with relationships at the workplace and having a high level of interpersonal "transaction" with many people during the course of the working day.

This is not a profile I would first associate with the product development or strategy roles that Lucinda had told me she was focusing on. This profile is more often associated with roles at the "boundary" of an organization such as sales, marketing, and business development. An internal product development role would be a good match only if certain conditions were met—for example, if it were in a managerial role in a busy environment within an organizational culture that valued the development of employees.

Lucinda went on to tell me about her interest in the retail industry. The first, and essentially only, job on her résumé was with the corporate headquarters of a leading retail apparel company. However, although it wasn't on her résumé, she had actually joined this company six years earlier as a salesperson. Early in her session she partially explained this omission when she related a traumatic experience from her first job at the corporate headquarters.

> "Something happened during my first few weeks at that corporate job. I was trying very hard to learn and to get

things right, and it was all new to me. It was scary. This was a busy place with a lot going on. I was excited because it was a "stretch," but I was also intimidated.

"When I was few weeks into the job, one of my coworkers, someone who'd been working there for several years, took me aside and told me that I was just not cutting it. I was devastated. I had thrown myself into it and was trying to make a place for myself there. So I redoubled my efforts to focus, learn the procedures, and not make mistakes. I was determined not to fail. I would do anything to get it right and to be accepted.

"I stuck to that job, but I was often bored. In the retail store, I never got bored. I had loved greeting customers and helping them. Sometimes they were rushed and they really needed something and I would zero in to understand what they wanted me to help them to get. I felt that I was really helping them. I enjoyed it.

"I like 'stretch work' that challenges me because I have never done it before and am not quite sure how to proceed. I get excited when I can be creative and have a challenge. But after I got through the first scary months there was no 'stretching' in that corporate setting."

Of the many things that can cause us to lose touch with the types of work that most interest us, fear is high on the list. The more I listened to Lucinda, the more I realized how traumatizing that experience in the inaugural weeks of her first corporate job had been. Her fear of repeating that near-failure was sidetracking Lucinda as she tried to imagine a job that would work for her. In the counseling session, I tried to help Lucinda focus on the "stretch" themes of excitement, uncertainty, and novelty while also considering the "safety" theme as well. I wanted her to acknowledge that their importance is not diminished by the dynamic tension they create within her.

> "You know, Lucinda, I wasn't going to talk about the tests," I said, picking up the printout of her assessment results, "but there's an important message here. Your highest basic interests are in the areas of Counseling and Mentoring and Influence Through Language and Ideas. These two areas, taken together, present a profile of someone for whom interaction with people is extraordinarily important. People with profiles like this want to be rubbing elbows with many different individuals throughout the day. They do not want to be stuck in a room by themselves or in front of a computer screen. They want to be 'at the boundary' of the work team, of the business unit, or of the whole organization—in roles in sales, marketing, or business development. If they are working on a more internally focused team, they need to be moving around and interacting with different teams and different people. Does this make sense to you?"

> Indeed it did.

> "So, in a way, Lucinda, you're pulled in two directions when you try to imagine the work that would be best for you. You like the liveliness and unpredictability of interacting spontaneously with people and working with the new issues that this brings up every day. But you also want to get things right, and to plan so that there are no

'messes' that could lead to the shaming experience that
you had in your very first corporate work experience.
Stretch and safety, spontaneity and planning. Can you
feel that tension? Once you have a good picture of these
two themes, Counseling and Mentoring and Influence
Through Language and Ideas, what other types of work
might fit the bill? Use them as a starting point for your
imagination, and use them also to test a particular job
opportunity, to make sure that it will give you what you
thrive on."

It is precisely in times of unusual stress that the hard work of
self-assessment pays off. If you know what is important for you, you
can more easily remember what counts, what you want, and the
types of situations that are most likely to provide it. You will be less
vulnerable to a "fight or flight" instinct based on what seems to offer
safety in the heat of a crisis. Like Lucinda, take the time to step back
and make important decisions based on knowledge that comes from
the core of your being.

Interests Versus Talents

In my conversations with clients, the question of talent inevitably
emerges. "I now know what I want," my client says, "but can I really
do it or is it just a fantasy?" The answer to that question, of course,
is that we cannot know without jumping into the pool and testing
our swimming muscles. At the same time, we know that talent ex-
ists, and it is particular. Objectively there are things that we can do
and things that we cannot. What can we say about this? How can we
come to know *our* special talents?

Over my years as a psychotherapist, career counselor, and organizational consultant, I have learned that the question of talent—some ineffable mix of skill, ability, intelligence, and affinity—is a loaded one. Our perceptions—and preconceptions—of talent are too often intertwined with sense of self. "What are you good at?" all too easily slides into "What good *are* you? Of what value are you?" These are difficult waters to navigate, particularly treacherous at key life transitions when we are most tempted to play judge when assessing our own accomplishments. So let us defy the culture's preoccupation with achievement and fame and do our best to separate talent from self-worth. Talent is not value; it is the adroit means through which we make our vision real, day by day. As a career progresses, exceptional skill will follow deeply embedded life interests. We get better and better at those things about which we are most excited. The first questions to consider are: What are my passions, and which roles will feed them?

Every operating manager I know who loves jumping every day into the thick of things with a team would feel spiritually bereft if she had to spend her day in front of a computer monitoring municipal bond credit ratings. Even after the buzz of the steep-learning honeymoon wears off, the person with highs on the Managing People and Relationships and Enterprise Control core functions will still thrill to the next team challenge. More important, she will be able to move on to develop much higher-level management skills precisely because she is excited about the challenges that come to someone in that role.

Likewise, the research engineer enthralled with a project that has brought him to the cutting edge of a technology would feel frustrated when interrupted (which is how he would experience it) by a subordinate needing supervisory guidance or a phone call from a key account. This engineer is likely to score high in Application of Technology and Theory Development and Conceptual Thinking, and have lower interest levels in Managing People and Relationships. He will remain excited with new theoretical and technical challenges, and feel most engaged in work environments that allow him to stay focused on these pursuits.

Regardless of our native general intelligence, our energy, and our ambition, we break through the level of good ability to exceptional ability in those areas that fundamentally excite us.

What to Do with Weakness

In my counseling work, I am often asked a related question: "Should I choose a job that I know I can do well, or one that will demand that I develop my weaknesses?" My answer is that life will give us plenty of opportunities to develop our weaknesses. We will not have the wherewithal to do so, however, if we are not operating from a core of strength. We need to look closely at the core requirements of a particular work role. Are they a good match for our deeply embedded life interests? We will have much to learn in *any* new setting, but do we have the necessary enthusiasm to gain a foothold in the first year on the job? If the answer to both of these questions is "yes," we should probably give the job serious consideration. If the answer is "no," we probably shouldn't.

The two biggest problems with developing strength in areas of skill weakness have nothing to do with finding the right "weakness opportunity." The first problem is having the honesty to know what our weaknesses actually are in more than an abstract way. It can be painful to focus on that which is awkward (or even embarrassing) and to acknowledge its existence. The second challenge is that we must be willing to tolerate the embarrassment of not knowing. We must be "shame hardy" in order to learn in areas where we do not have native ability. Meeting these two challenges is difficult enough. If we deliberately accept a job that "plays to our weaknesses" we are unlikely to have the composure to self-observe and the courage to make mistakes.

George Anastasi is now in his seventies and has had a long and successful career in sales. In terms of deeply embedded life interests, George scores high on the Counseling and Mentoring, Managing People and Relationships, and Influence Through Language and Ideas core functions. He has notably low scores in the Application of Technology, Creative Production, and Quantitative Analysis core functions. This pattern suggests that George is a "people person" who will probably enjoy direct management roles. His average or lower Creative Production and Enterprise Control interests suggest that he prefers structured work environments, perhaps in a large company.

George graduated from business school and went to work as a salesperson for a huge multinational consumer-products company. He excelled and was promoted to sales manager, regional sales manager, and ultimately vice president of sales for a division of the company. He built his reputation as a people-oriented manager: He was highly skilled at building customer relationships and an effective team leader. He was not an accomplished analyst or strategist. He genuinely enjoyed the interactive aspect of business, and this abiding passion—and the consequent skills he developed in this area—fueled his success.

Naomi Fleischer is a much more recent business school graduate than George and might be the yang to his yin. Her personal high core function scores are in Application of Technology, Quantitative

Analysis, and Enterprise Control. She has notably low scores in Counseling and Mentoring, Managing People and Relationships, and Influence Through Language and Ideas. Naomi joined a management consulting firm after graduating and quickly earned a reputation for being a star analyst and strategic thinker. In the consulting world, however, that is only half of the story. She was frankly much less interested in negotiating the organizational politics of client companies, team management, and anticipating opportunities to sell new business. When she transferred to internal consulting in a large package delivery company, she was much more effective—and happier. There she was operating as a solo consultant out of the office of a very senior executive, which minimized the importance of skill in the areas of politics, team dynamics, and sales.

DEEP DIVE

Remembering Who You Are

As you read this chapter, your understanding of your two or three most important deeply embedded life interests can become more detailed and specific. Here are some exercises to help:

First, recall the time in your life when your daily activities were best aligned with these themes. Where were you living and what were you doing? Were your interests being expressed both at work and in your personal life? What specific activities, at work and outside of work, were most rewarding?

Next, recall a time when you consciously made a major work or nonwork commitment that had little to do with your most

Both George and Naomi eventually developed centers of skill competence related to work roles that were fed by their interests. (See "Deep Dive: Remembering Who You Are.") But both needed to enhance less developed skill areas. George needed to work on analytical and strategic skills and Naomi on political and interpersonal skills. But each did this development outward from a center of strength. That center remained the key element of their identity within the organization. Once that identity and the contributions that it brought to the organization were recognized, it was easier to take the risks necessary to venture into less familiar terrain.

There is indeed more to who we are than our deepest passions: there are values that are passed down to us and made our own after much struggle. Knowing what deeply moves us is, at least, a place

important deeply embedded life interests. What compelled you to make this choice? How long did it take you to realize that things were not right? What were the symptoms or warning signs?

Finally, look at your current work and life situations. Now that you know the two or three most important themes of your deeply embedded life interests, how would you assess the opportunity you have to express them in your daily life? Do the core demands of your job call on the "fuel" of these passions? Outside of work, do you deliberately make choices and select activities that offer a great chance to express these interests? In your current situation are you closer to living from your deepest interests or further away? What changes might you make, at work and in your life, to allow these interests to find greater expression on a daily basis? Be as specific as possible.

to begin and a place to return to when we find ourselves wanting another life. Søren Kierkegaard spoke of the "despair of wanting to be another self"; we all know that despair.[1] At times of such despair, knowing what it is that moves us the most can be a critical touchstone. Tapping the source of our greatest enthusiasm can lead us back to the path toward a place that feels like *our* place, where we can stand and offer something that, over time, becomes *our* contribution.

Our contribution, however, can only be realized in a specific social context. We always live out our vision with others who are striving to live theirs. The next step is learning to recognize patterns that point to the way in which our passion and our vision find a home within organizations and within the human community.

SEVEN

Power, People, and Achievement

Three Interwoven Patterns

SAMANTHA MCPHERSON, now thirty-five, was born and raised in California but has spent the last decade working in Europe. She is a warm and outgoing person who listens well and cares about what others have to say. She has worked in nonprofit organizations her entire life, mostly in higher education. When I met her, she was an assistant director in the office of student life at a prominent European university. Sam had come to one of my workshops because she was facing an impasse.

"I spent the first five years after the birth of my children doing part-time contract work in order to dedicate myself to nurturing my two beautiful baby girls," she said by way of explaining her interest. "Over time, I found myself increasingly restless and intellectually bored. When I found the opportunity to work at the university, it fulfilled so many of my dream job criteria that I went back full time even though I never planned to be a working mom. Altruism is an important motivator for me and I feel I am making a real difference for the students. I also enjoy working in a busy office with other people. Plus, I found in the university's internationalism a home for my own eclectic personal history.

"Now I feel stuck. Our director is leaving and the search committee for her job has approached me. They see me as serious candidate to lead the office, but they need to know if I am open to taking on all of the responsibility that comes with the director role, and they need to know soon. I find myself torn. I am a bit surprised at how much the idea of being the boss appeals to me. But I know I'll have to put in a lot more hours if I take the job. What do I really want?"

Over the years in my work as a psychotherapist, researcher, and career counselor I have come to appreciate the central role that three social needs (or social "motivators") play in our life decisions: the need to act in our immediate world, the need to belong, and the need to achieve. A shorthand to expression of these three needs is: power, people, and achievement.[1] For some of us, one of the three is clearly dominant and accounts for most of our social decision making. For others, two may vie closely for prominence, and our behaviors in groups will alternate between choices that fulfill first one and then the other. Very few of us have an even balance of all three, but recognizing our particular pattern of emphasis will tell us much about our social motivations in work and in life.

Power: The Ability to Act

The first way to consider power is in its broadest sense. Aristotle's view of power, as the ability to act, remains the most simple and elegant. We all want to be actors on the stage of our lives; we all want the power we need to perform. Some of us are more clear about the power we want and more comfortable in the pursuit of it; all of us need to develop a realistic sense of what we need to do to get what we want. We need to know how much focus and intensity to bring to the pursuit of our goal.

The word power typically conjures up images of what is more accurately described as positional or formal power: the CEO of the large corporation or the cabinet-level government minister. Power, however, has many manifestations. The power of the poet is different from the power of the politician, which in turn is different from the power of a spiritual guru. In *Kinds of Power*, psychologist James Hillman explored the ways in which power is evident in the human world. He uses the words "authority" and "control," which are perhaps most readily associated with power, in chapter titles. The titles of some of his other chapters, however, bring home the point that the essence of power is more varied and subtle than we first imagine:

- **Prestige:** Power that is inferred merely by affiliation with well-regarded institutions or traditions

- **Exhibitionism:** The willingness to draw attention to ourselves in a dramatic or unusual fashion, even if ephemeral

- **Ambition:** Raw drive and determination

- **Reputation:** Being known as reliable or as having certain admired qualities

- **Influence:** The particular power of being close to and trusted by others who are in a position to act

- **Resistance:** Being an underdog advocate of a just or morally compelling cause, such as Mahatma Gandhi and Martin Luther King, Jr.

- **Leadership:** The ability, even in those who are young or lack positional authority, to truly inspire and attract followers

- **Charisma:** The gift of inspiring others simply through physical presence

- **Fearsomeness:** The use of fear to accomplish objectives[2]

Power indeed comes to us in different ways. Both the aboriginal adolescent on a vision quest for a guiding spirit and the college freshman considering a major are straining to glimpse the power that will allow them to act in the world. Power is that which allows each individual to be unique and, at the same time, a valued contributor to the collective. When we talk about someone "at the height of her power," we may just as easily be talking about a novelist or tennis player as a senator or general. We might even say that each of us has our own unique manifestation of power that we grow into as we grow up. We can speak of human development as an individual's discovery of a particular way of being effective in the world, the development of her specific powers. (See "Deep Dive: Your Power.")

DEEP DIVE

Your Power

Consider the following sentence: "We might even say that each of us has our own unique manifestation of power that we grow into as we grow up." What do you know about power, your particular ways of being effective, of getting what you need and want? Pause now, and with your free attention, look at the associations that come to mind as you read that sentence.

The Alpha Type

When it comes to understanding how our need for power affects our happiness in particular jobs, we must focus on one particular aspect of power, the need for dominance.

For individuals with a high need for dominance, the exercise of power becomes a goal in itself. They typically define the standard for sufficient power contextually as the opportunity to be a *dominant actor*. They want to be an agent in both their immediate and, to the extent that it is possible, broader working environments. These people find it difficult to imagine they could perform meaningful work in a situation where they are not significant "players" or decision makers.

As in animal communities, there are in the human community individuals who have a strong drive for dominance, or "Alpha" types. In Alphas the need for dominance takes precedence over the two other social orientations (people and achievement) we are considering, and they will look for the shortest route possible to positions

Take the time to do some brief spontaneous writing on the images of your power.

What would your parents and siblings say about your power? How did you get your way in your family of origin?

How would your spouse, partner, or best friend describe your powers?

How did your boss talk about your effectiveness in your last performance review?

Take the time to reflect more deeply, and honestly, on how you make things happen.

of authority. When assessing our own need for dominance we can look at three things: past career decision making; the language we use when talking about specific career goals, and the people whom we admire.

Of these three, past career decision making is perhaps the most transparent. Even as far back as high school, we might find that we sought power in roles such as class officer, officer of clubs, team captain, and participation in political campaigns. We can look to the future by asking ourselves an open-ended question such as, "What do I want to be doing in five to seven years?" The Alpha person's answer will always emphasize authority: "I want to be leading . . ., I want to be running . . ., I want to be in charge of . . ., I want to have my own . . ." These are all situations where the primary consideration is power itself. Of course, every description of the future vision will contain some aspect of enhanced power and increased ability to command the resources necessary to achieve goals, but when Alpha individuals describe their future lives, the acquisition of power is paramount.

Alphas often present themselves in a dominant fashion. They take the lead in meetings or in dinner-party conversations, often having a well-articulated agenda. They are often highly task-oriented and may give the impression of being impatient. Their gestures are pointed, their manner direct, their voices full and confident. Some Alphas clothe their high-dominance, warrior-like essence in the silk of self-restraint and graciousness. Unlike their less mature Alpha associates, they can patiently listen to others and give measured responses, rarely betraying an urgent need for closure.

We all have a need for power, even a need for dominance, at some level. For some of us, upbringing and conscious or unconscious messages from influential people in our lives suggested that expressing power needs was unacceptable. Others among us have been given the green light to value the quest for power. For many, acknowledging power needs, perhaps for the first time, is an important step in claiming more satisfying work and life situations.

Tempered Dominance

Even those who know Sam McPherson fairly well do not regard her as a power-oriented person. They have found she is more likely to describe the events in the lives of her four- and six-year-old daughters than organizational politics. And the results of her One Hundred Jobs exercise suggest this perception is not completely wrong. Here are Sam's top twelve choices (Sam used an earlier version of this exercise; the wording of her choices sometimes differs from the wording of the current version in this book):

1. Fiction writer

2. Director of an academic department (instead of the service department where I am now)

3. Diplomat

4. Judge

5. Mayor of a city or town

6. Architect

7. Professor

8. Religious counselor

9. Psychotherapist

10. Armed services officer

11. Ship captain

12. Music composer

Although this is not a blatantly power-driven list, Sam did choose four power-oriented roles (director of an academic department, mayor of a city or town, armed services officer, ship captain) and two others (diplomat and judge) that have power shadings. An analysis of her One Hundred Jobs exercise revealed to Sam that Enterprise Control belonged among her life interest personal highs along with Counseling and Mentoring and Influence Through Language and Ideas. Although she does not present herself to the world as an Alpha type, she has become more able to acknowledge her desire for power and to realize that she wants ultimately to find a work role that will allow for its expression.

Shortly after the workshop ended, Sam made her decision:

"I now realize that I really do strive to be in a position of authority working together with a group of people I respect," she told me. "I want to solve problems and add value to peoples' lives. I also want to raise my children well, with all my heart and soul; in fact, this is the single most important thing that I do with my life. But this does not completely fulfill my life's plan, and I think there's more I'm supposed to do. (I am strongly religious and I'd like to think I have an active relationship with God—trying to figure out what it is He wants me to do here for Him.)

"I was offered my boss's position and turned it down. I now know it's the right decision, although it was very hard at the time. Why was it right? Because my most important value, lifestyle balance, is being met in my current job where I have additional time off to be with my kids throughout the year."

Sam made the choice appropriate to that particular moment in her life, but it will be interesting to see whether her desire for power leads her to take on more leadership responsibility as her children grow and her attention is again drawn to potential contributions in the workplace.

Humanity cannot be neatly divided into low-need-for-dominance and high-need-for-dominance individuals. But it is possible to get a sense of the strength of an individual's need for dominance and the extent to which this need colors both career vision and interpersonal style. (See "Deep Dive: Need for Dominance.") For those of us with a stronger orientation toward the interpersonal realm or the realm of achievement, it is important to weigh the role power may play in our getting where we want to go. We need to say to ourselves, "Let's be realistic, what's it really going to take to get there?"

Alpha individuals are often high in Enterprise Control and, like Controllers, prone to shooting themselves in the foot, particularly in the first two or three years of their careers. Controllers want to lead, to manage, to be players; that is, they want a lot of responsibility and the ability to act and make decisions. It is safe to say that they will not get as much of this as they would like early on. If their frustration with this comes off as arrogance, insensitivity, lack of respect, or general power hunger, they will probably raise doubts about their ability to be evenhanded, patient, and sensitive in professional relationships. If we are Controllers, we need to watch out for this, to get feedback from confidants. We need to learn that ambition and a desire for taking leadership roles are to be valued highly but are most effectively realized when restraint, empathy, and interpersonal sensitivity are also strongly in evidence.

Outside of work, if we have a dominant power orientation, we will look for opportunities for leadership and influence in family and community settings. Spearheading major initiatives for charitable organizations, taking on leadership roles on school and other community boards, being officers in professional organizations, or

Need for Dominance

Reread the definition of power at the beginning of the chapter. How would you rate the strength of your need for dominance? Are you clear and comfortable with your power needs? Is your need for power stronger than your need for relationships (affiliation) and achievement?

You can use the results of the One Hundred Jobs exercise to help you in this assessment. Did you choose many of these work roles: chief executive officer, ship captain, chief financial officer, investment banker, entrepreneur, venture capitalist, elected public official, mayor of a city or town, senior manager of a manufacturing business, diplomat, and litigator (courtroom lawyer)? Even a few of these present on your list indicate a significant need for dominance orientation. However, the best measure of the strength

fund-raising for colleges or graduate schools are likely to be attractive opportunities.

People: The Need to Belong

We all long for satisfying relationships. In human culture, such needs are met through coworkers, families, religious groups, social networks, and our neighborhoods and larger communities. We can learn about our needs for affiliation by listening carefully to the way in which we portray the importance of the interpersonal realm of your need for dominance must await your tallying the number of work role choices for both the achievement and affiliation dimensions. It is the *relative* weighting of the three orientations that is most important.

If you have participated in my Image Gathering exercise on the Web, the information from that experience can help you analyze your need for dominance. In how many of the images were you in charge or running the show? In your response to "Who does the work of your vision?" were your heroes people known in an obvious way for their power orientation?

Is Enterprise Control as a personal high among your basic life interests? When you consider a job opportunity, do you place a strong emphasis on title, authority, or opportunity to rapidly advance to positions of greater authority?

All of these observations are indicators of the strength of your need for dominance.

when we talk about our lives. We can also look for the times we make choices based on interpersonal considerations.

Do we talk spontaneously about the type of people we want to work with? Can we easily describe experiences where otherwise interesting work was undermined by an estrangement from colleagues or a culture that did not value connection and cooperation? Do we pursue roles that offer lots of interpersonal contact on a daily basis? When we describe our career vision or previous experiences, do affiliation themes emerge as frequently or more frequently than themes related to need for dominance and need for achievement? Is

DEEP DIVE

Need for Affiliation

What do you know about your need for affiliation? Is it more or less important than your need for dominance? For achievement? The following work roles from the One Hundred Jobs exercise are typically associated with affiliation (individuals in these work roles may also, of course, have significant or even relatively higher orientations on the power and achievement dimensions as well): sports coach, salesperson in a retail store, social services professional, psychotherapist, public relations professional, TV talk show host, speech therapist, religious counselor, director of human resources, high school teacher, director of nonprofit organization, real estate salesperson, nurse, and homemaker. Four or more of

the *relational* aspect of life as important or more important for us than what is sometimes referred to as the *agentic* (goal-oriented or power-oriented) aspect of life?

If we have a high need for affiliation we will seek work roles requiring much interaction with many people during the course of the day. We will want these roles to include interaction with people outside of our immediate team or even outside of our organization itself. Sales, marketing, business development, and public relations are obvious examples of such roles, but any role in which the relationship component is central will offer the opportunity for a good match. (See "Deep Dive: Need for Affiliation.")

these work roles on your top twelve list would be indicative of a significant affiliation orientation.

Think now about the images that came to you in the Image Gathering exercise. Did many of them involve interacting with people? Were you on the move, meeting many people during the course of the exercise? Did the interactions involve your listening as much as your speaking?

Do you have deeply embedded life interest personal highs on Counseling and Mentoring or Managing People and Relationships? (Both of these dimensions correlate with an affiliation orientation.)

Think about your work situation. Do you look forward to the relationships that you have there? Have you or would you base a job choice on the people you would be working with every day? Would you place the people value proposition of a job above moderate differences in title, intellectual challenge, or compensation?

Outside Work:
Belonging to a Community

Outside of work, if affiliation is a dominant social motivator for us, we will place a strong value on spending time with family and friends. We will be more likely to make career compromises that enable us to devote ourselves to family or to invest time in organizations that foster fellowship. Although we may be a leader in these organizations, the value of social belonging will be as strong as, if not stronger than, the motivation of being an influential decision maker. (See "Deep Dive: Affiliation in the Social Context.")

DEEP DIVE

Affiliation in the Social Context

What are you willing to sacrifice in terms of career development in order to protect time and energy for family and friendships?

Outside of work, are your affiliation needs met by a wide circle of friends or by a smaller circle of more intimate friends?

Compare yourself to three people you know well (choose them now, just as they come to mind) in terms of your willingness to trade off achievement and power (career advancement) goals for the sake of greater time spent with family and friends. Where among the three do you fall?

Do this exercise again with another set of three people you know well. Are the results similar?

Achievement: The Desire to Accomplish

We often associate achievement with ascension in a particular organizational hierarchy, but this notion is actually more closely related to power. Achievement for our purposes refers to the need to accomplish, independent of the consequences of accomplishment within an organization. Think of the scientist laboring for years at her laboratory bench and gaining pleasure from the publication of her findings in journals read by a tiny scientific audience. Think of a design engineer who has no aspirations for a management role putting in the extra hours in his attempt to achieve a new product breakthrough. Think of the concert violinist practicing for hours for the love of the beauty of the music she makes. These individuals are driven to achieve independent of their desire for power. For those who crave achievement, accomplishment is an end in itself.

The drive to achieve finds perhaps its purest expression in the worlds of art and science. But business professionals also crave some aspect of accomplishment, even if their need for power or for affiliation is a primary career motivator. I have found it useful to talk about three distinct achievement dimensions: challenge, learning, and authorship. These categories overlap, but considering them individually allows us to reflect more deeply on just what achievement means to each of us.

Challenge

Some people experience achievement primarily as one of two types of challenge: *personal* challenge and *competitive* challenge. (Both, though, may be present for any given individual.) Personal challenge boils down to taking one's ability to the next level. People motivated in this fashion strive for their "personal best." Adding an extra inch to the high-jump bar, even if the track competitor knows she will not win the event; increasing his results by 20 percent over the previous quarter, even if the sales associate has no chance to be top salesperson; publishing an article for the first time even if the writer has no intention of penning a second: these are examples of a personal challenge, centered on goals that promise self-improvement. Another name for personal challenge is *mastery*. The concert pianist who works for months to master a difficult piece challenges herself to master a certain skill and to achieve a certain level of artistry.

The need to meet personal challenges may exist largely independent of financial reward or competition with others. But competitive challenge has everything to do with besting others. Being the manager of the month; pulling the all-nighter to deliver the presentation

Personal Best or Best in Show?

When you talk about challenge, do you more often use the language of personal challenge or the language of competitive challenge? For you, is challenge a sense of energy, enthusiasm, and yearning that comes more from a "personal best" story or more from a "beat the other team" story? Perhaps both have meaning for you and occur in relative balance.

that puts the others to shame; beating the other tennis team: these are challenges with a center of gravity that lies outside of the self. In this case, we experience accomplishment relative to the performance of others. Many managers are much more ready to define, encourage, and recognize competitive challenge than personal challenge. Different work roles are also likely to reward one orientation more than the other. (See "Deep Dive: Personal Best or Best in Show?")

Learning

A common complaint from people looking for a career transition is "I am no longer learning anything new" or "I want to learn more." Sometimes, the person is defining learning in a very practical sense; they are really saying, "I have a definite career goal in mind and I must acquire specific skills to be competitive for such a position, but I do not have the opportunity to acquire such skills in my current position." Not as often but not infrequently either, such complaints come from individuals who simply love to learn and feel most connected with their work when they must master a new area of knowledge.

I can still see the excitement in the face of the young MBA student who told me, "I had never done it before and there was no one there to tell me what to do. They simply said, 'Get it done,' and I had to learn as much as I could as fast as I could." This student was not a natural academic (though a certain number of academic stars, or those with a passion for esoteric knowledge, find their way into business school), but she was thrilled by the acquisition of new knowledge. Whether the goal is practical application or erudition, for people like this student an important part of what truly feels like achievement is learning.

Authorship

For some people, authorship provides the opportunity to extend the recognition of their accomplishments beyond the immediate working environment. In addition to actual writing, publication, or patent registration, authorship may include any activity aimed at the building, over time, of a personal "brand" that extends recognition beyond the boundaries of one's own organization. This dimension of achievement has gained greater importance as careers have become less tightly tethered to particular organizations. Many professionals now evaluate a prospective job in terms of what success in that position will add to the portfolio of achievements they will take with them as they move on to different settings.

Others have little interest in building a personal brand. Instead, they experience achievement in the recognition they receive from a specific community, regardless of their position within the power hierarchy of that community. For these people, being the recognized expert or the "go-to" person is in itself the reward. They might be the leader of a yoga group, the family historian within an extended clan, or the gourmet everyone turns to for advice and recipes at Thanksgiving.

If achievement is our dominant social motivator, we will need to learn or to be challenged in all aspects of life. We will probably pursue areas of expertise that are independent of our professional calling, becoming, for example, an expert in the history of World War II, an opera buff, or a builder of traditional wooden boats. Athletics is a common arena for accomplishment among achievement-dominant individuals. (See "Deep Dive: Dimensions of Achievement.")

In the next chapter, we will look at the way that our needs for power, achievement, and affiliation work together as a dynamic triad. We will also see how they contribute to the overall "map" of our personality.

DEEP DIVE

Dimensions of Achievement

The achievement dimensions of challenge, learning, and authorship are not discrete. There is often overlap between two or more of the dimensions. Take some time now to reflect and imagine. Over the past twelve months, what did you do that made you feel most strongly that you had "really done something"?

Imagine forward to one year from now. At the end of the next twelve months, what would make you feel that you have done "real work" and made a genuine contribution?

Look at your answers to both questions and consider which of the three dimensions of achievement, or which combination, seem to be most important for you.

Achievement is very content-specific. A scientist achieves and a painter achieves and an athlete achieves. Individual contributor roles tend to be achievement-oriented. When working with the list of work roles from the One Hundred Jobs exercise that are typically associated with a high achievement, exercise caution. The contents of many achievement-oriented roles may not appeal to you in and of themselves. That doesn't mean you don't have a high need to accomplish. In one sense, every one of the one hundred work roles could attract achievement-dominant individuals.

If you participated in the Image Gathering exercise, analyze what it says about your need for achievement. Look at how many of your images involved developing, completing, or launching a tangible product. Also look at how many involved achieving an unambiguously measurable goal such as publishing a book, finishing a painting, obtaining a patent, making a scientific discovery, accomplishing a sales goal, or meeting an important deadline or target.

EIGHT

Mapping Our Insights

Patterns in the Sand

I N DECIDING whether to take the leadership role in her university department, Samantha McPherson considered what she knew about herself. She knew that her most important life interests are Influence through Language and Ideas, Counseling and Mentoring, and Enterprise Control. She also has significant interests associated with Creative Production. Affiliation is her highest social motivator, followed by power; her pure achievement needs are significantly weaker. This pattern suggests that Sam had done well to seek out work in an organization that had a strong social mission (allowing her to realize her Counseling and Mentoring interests) and to immerse herself amid a busy, service-oriented staff that shared her sense of social mission (satisfying her primary affiliation orientation). If Sam were to take this insight about her deeply embedded life interests and social motivators and add to it the themes and dynamic tensions that emerged from her One Hundred Jobs and Image Gathering exercises, the "map" of her career and life vision would look like figure 8-1.

Although Sam made a temporary lifestyle choice in turning down the director role, the analysis of her workshop exercises helped her to envision where she needed to go next to achieve greater satisfaction. In the short term, she needed to develop and lead student programs that would allow her to express her Persuader interests. In the longer term, when her family commitments would allow it, she knew that leadership roles would be essential, given her the strength of her Boss interests and her subtle but important need for power.

FIGURE 8-1

Sam's map

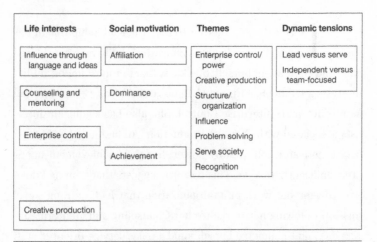

Life interests	Social motivation	Themes	Dynamic tensions
Influence through language and ideas	Affiliation	Enterprise control/ power	Lead versus serve
		Creative production	Independent versus team-focused
Counseling and mentoring	Dominance	Structure/ organization	
		Influence	
Enterprise control		Problem solving	
	Achievement	Serve society	
		Recognition	
Creative production			

So far, we have learned how to analyze the profile of our deeply embedded life interests and how to extract our major work and life themes from the One Hundred Jobs and Image Gathering exercises. We must now learn how to analyze our social motivators. Our respective needs for power, people, and achievement, if recognized and fed, can serve as potent motivators in our lives, making a big difference in our feelings of fulfillment and contentment. When we combine this knowledge with what we have learned about our themes, life interests, and dynamic tensions, we can step back and look at the broader pattern in the carpet of our lives.

The Triad

When it comes to need for dominance, affiliation, and accomplishment, what we need to know is: What is the main source of our social motivation? Which element of the power, people, and achievement triad provides the lodestar for decisions about the activities that will be most interesting and the kinds of groups or organizations that will be most attractive?

It is too simplistic to label anyone as a "power person," a "people person," or an "achievement person." We must instead assess the relationship between the primary social motivator and the remaining two social motivators, which temper that primary orientation. To chart our own social-motivation paradigm, we start by identifying our primary motivator. Then we place each of the two remaining social motivators at the proper distance from our primary motivator and from each other.

The two diagrams in figure 8-2 represent two people with very different social motivations. On the left is the pattern of an individual who has a strong motivational need for dominance and a significant secondary achievement orientation. (The diagrams for ambitious business leaders or presidents of volunteer boards would have similar patterns.) On the right is the pattern of an individual who is more likely to define success—in work or life—in terms of relationships and achievements than hierarchical power. (Longtime staff writers at magazines and community activists who provide gourmet meals for championship teams or the local theater troupe would likely diagram their triads in this way.)

If we are Alpha types who have a high need for dominance, we will want to obtain as much formal and informal authority as possible. We see the world in terms of hierarchies and construe career development as movement in as direct a path as possible toward progressively higher positions. For us, meaningful work is the continuing effort to extend our ability to act and be influential. Alpha types typically define intelligence, consciously or unconsciously, as the ability to discern the locus and flow of power within and between organizations and to maneuver to be in the right places and develop the right connections. Powerful figures, either in history or in the world around them, are the Alphas' heroes and role models. If this is us, we are far more likely, when asked whom we admire, to

FIGURE 8-2

Two different social motivation patterns

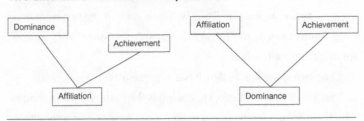

mention famous politicians, celebrity CEOs, or prominent social leaders than accomplished scientists or artists.

Some of us, like Raymond Becker from chapter 2, are Alpha individuals who also have a high need for achievement—and a history of notable accomplishments even early in our lives. We may keep up our violin practice or train hard for the next marathon, but our real focus is on moving toward positions of greater authority. The need for achievement may be strong for us, but it is secondary.

Those of us who are Alpha types vary considerably in the way we relate to the people around us. As leaders, some of us will want to be around people every day and will want to affect others, even if our need for affiliation is low in comparison to our need for dominance. We can also be highly altruistic, and may even measure our power in terms of what we see as the total number of people our exercise of this power has "helped." On the other hand, some Alpha leaders experience power as the ability to acquire and effectively deploy abstract assets, financial or otherwise; for us, *people* do not prominently figure into our experience of that power. For example, the manager of a busy service business has a very different sense of power than the successful investment manager who controls several billion dollars worth of assets but spends most of his time talking to a few trusted associates.

Consider a comparison between Oprah Winfrey and Bill Gates. Winfrey has clearly set her sights on influencing as wide an audience as possible. But her power comes from her relationship with her audience, and she experiences it as something that is derived from both the quality and extension of that relationship. Gates, by contrast, has obtained and exercised his power—also with undeniable success—at a higher level of abstraction. His genius for understanding both technology and the dynamics of markets has made him one of the most influential business leaders of his time. But we don't get the sense that he has a high need for interpersonal transaction. (And he clearly is motivated by the competitive challenge of besting the likes of Novell, Netscape, and Google.)

This has nothing to do with Gates's values or his sense of altruism; he is emerging as one of the most effective philanthropists of our time. It does have to do, however, with how he defines power, and for him that definition does not seem to have a strong interpersonal context.

So if analyses of our life experiences, our Image Gathering, and our One Hundred Jobs exercises point to a high power orientation, do we stand on the Oprah Winfrey side of the spectrum or on the Bill Gates side in the *interpersonal* world? We need to ask ourselves what types of organizations and paths to power will bring us the greatest satisfaction.

Those of us who have a dominant achievement motivation (Achievers) often focus on "excellence." The most parsimonious computer program, the breakthrough microchip design, the record sales number, the novel that brings critical acclaim, the new model that enables clients to better understand their markets are all experiences that are inherently more meaningful for us than *managing* the software or computer hardware company, being a college dean, or being the CEO of the company facing a difficult challenge in the marketplace. For those of us who are Achievers, accomplishment and excellence simply *mean* more than power and control.

As Achievers we may find ourselves in roles of authority, but when we do so it is often an unintended consequence of our actions. The successful scientist is promoted to project manager, the successful newspaper reporter advances to editor, the successful teacher becomes a principal, or the classy waiter is made maître d'— all rise in the hierarchy because of their excellence. But we must be aware of the difference between the power-oriented leader and the achievement-oriented individual who finds herself in a position of power. The Achiever often has trouble making the transition to management because the challenge of the technical work still holds its fascination. He knows how to do it well, perhaps better than any of the people who he now manages, and it is hard for them not to get involved in the details of staff members' work.

Truth be told, the details often hold more *meaning* for those of us who are Achievers, and we may lack the basic instinct for power and how it moves within an organization. We must exert great effort to build alliances, cultivate influence, and defuse resistance, which often leads to frustration at the energy taken away from "the real work." Meanwhile, this is the very stuff that the power-dominant Alpha lives and breathes. The advantages of an Alpha person in this realm are obvious. If we are Achievers we must make the extra effort; some of us will take to it and others won't. (Those of us who do probably have a strong secondary power orientation.)

If we are clearly excited about the challenges of functional expertise and are obviously oriented toward achieving excellence in our discipline, where we are on the power dimension may determine our place in the hierarchy. The combination of high achievement and low power orientations is a recipe for the teacher, engineer, or designer who either remains in an individual contributor role or returns to the individual contributor role after a foray into management. Others are able to take on a management role and see it as an extension of their accomplishment.

The person with a dominant need for affiliation, the Connector, is strongly oriented toward the organizational culture and the personalities of coworkers. Connectors are keenly attuned to the social dimension of work, which does not necessarily imply the opportunity to develop a network of friends but rather an appreciation for the interpersonal content of the work itself. In a work setting we Connectors seek community, knowing that we will spend much of our waking lives within this community. We value a team orientation and are good team players. We look for managers who are genuinely committed to the development of the people within the organization. We favor a culture of respect, congeniality, and higher levels of interpersonal interaction. Work cultures that are highly formal—where communication up and down the hierarchy is limited—will be problematic for us. Also problematic will be working environments that require extensive periods of time in relative isolation.

If, like Samantha, we are Connectors with an at least moderate need for power, we often choose to develop careers as managers, but managers who place an emphasis on team dynamics. We value individual differences and try to harness those differences to achieve high productivity based on inherent employee satisfaction. Obviously, Connectors will be more satisfied in an organization that supports this style of management than one that does not.

On the other hand, if we are Connectors with low power needs, we will typically be uncomfortable in more aggressive, "star-oriented" cultures characterized by conflict and competition. When push comes to shove, we dislike both pushing and shoving. We prefer to preserve a relationship than to sacrifice it in order to achieve optimal efficiency for the task at hand. We need to learn, if we're going to aspire to management roles, that being direct and demanding, and even requesting behavioral change, can lead to growth and a larger repertoire, both for ourselves and for the people we manage. We need to learn that becoming more efficient and results-oriented does not necessarily require becoming more cynical or insensitive.

Which is your primary social motivator? (See "Deep Dive: The Power, People, and Achievement Triad.")

DEEP DIVE

The Power, People, and Achievement Triad

How would you graph your own profile of these key social motivators? Would you have drawn the same diagram five or ten years ago? Do your current work and life settings provide a good context for these motivators? If not, can you imagine settings that would?

Mapping Our Patterns

Carol Weil, a graphic artist in Boston, is much in demand. When she is in the room, one is very aware of her presence. Although not a large person, she commands the space around her; she has an athletic bearing and her body flows in graceful movements. Her eyes are sharp and sparkling, and she keeps solid eye contact with whomever she is speaking. Her mind always seems busy analyzing and reflecting, and her words, while carefully chosen, are spoken with ease. She loves to talk and can speak with quiet intimacy or an entertaining boom.

At age thirty-five, Carol found herself at a difficult impasse. She had just returned from a trip to Scotland with her father, sister, and brother, as well as her stepmother and half-sister. Family has always been extraordinarily important for her; she had always made great efforts to keep in touch with her brother and sister and cultivate a relationship with her stepmother. Carol had anticipated the trip with great enthusiasm.

In reality, however, the trip turned out to be both confusing and upsetting. Carol and her brother Michael, age thirty-three, constantly competed for their father's attention. Carol remarked, "No sooner had we arrived in Edinburgh and rented a car, then my brother got behind the wheel and drove us to St Andrews. He, my father, and my half-sister would get up early and head out to the golf course. Because of knee injuries, I could not join them, but rather visited cultural spots with my stepmother. I felt left out. At dinner, the jockeying for my father's attention usually resulted in conversation in which I was teased relentlessly, and sometimes brutally, by my stepmother, brother, and sister. I found myself going for long walks and crying uncontrollably. I ended up getting a nasty flu that kept me largely bedridden for the second week of the trip." The trip that was supposed to be a chance for time with adult siblings became, in subtle and not-so-subtle ways, a struggle both in daily interactions and, more importantly, in the tumult of emotions sweeping through Carol.

When Carol returned to Boston she felt that she simply did not know what had happened or what she wanted to happen next. She had always thought of herself as someone who put family above all else, but now she was not sure what she would say to any of them, parents or siblings alike, in their next conversation. In the course of working through her impasse, Carol was able to reflect more deeply on her family experience growing up.

Carol's parents had divorced when she was a teenager, and she and her siblings had spent time in the new households of both parents. "One of the first things I came to realize was that I had two separate family constellations, and I had always played very different roles in each," she commented. "With my mother and my two full siblings, I was the eldest, the star achiever, the one who looked out for my brother and sister, and the one my mother relied on. My two high social motivators—people and achievement—were allowed to thrive; my mother (who didn't trust her often errant son) gave me a strong power role.

"With my father and stepmother, my brother—the only son and, as the third Michael Weil, my father's namesake in spades—was given (and seized) the dominant power role. In the jockeying for attention, my achievements were often mocked. (Since my achievements were the cause of loving attention from my father, they therefore made my stepmother and siblings quite jealous.) I would invest a lot of my affiliation energy trying to get along with everyone, but I often felt foiled by the competitive crosscurrents.

"Once I realized that a lot of the pain came from power struggles with my brother and half-sister, I realized that these were struggles that I didn't even *want* to engage in. I had never really needed to be top dog, but rather had accepted the role my mother had given me. When I realized that I could just relax and let my brother be the Alpha, a palpable sense of relief came over me. I could feel it in my body. When my half-sister struggled for attention, I tried to be patient and supportive.

"Later, when I told my dad and stepmom about how I always felt attacked by my brother and half-sister, my stepmother astutely pointed out that I was more like my father than I realized, and that this frustrated my siblings. I slowly came to realize how much I shared my father's drive, passions, and personality. I was able to carve out time alone with him when we could enjoy going to the theater together, sharing good books, or taking hikes in the woods, where we'd compare notes on management styles. This so satisfied my desire to connect that it lessened my need to compete for his attention at the dinner table. There I could lean back, relax, and let one of the others take over."

In her counseling work, Carol completed a number of assessments, including the One Hundred Jobs exercise. Her career and life vision map shown in figure 8-3.

Carol realized that power had never really been an authentic motivator for her. She felt much more connected and in the flow when operating from her achievement passions in her professional projects and from her affiliation needs, both at work and in her personal life. Her mistaken and unconscious notion that she had to seek and succeed in power roles, had, over the years, been a source of both emotional pain and career misdirection. She had worked hard to become the manager of a graphic arts studio, only to learn the hard way that her real passion was in the artwork itself. Her recent years as a freelance artist have been among her happiest and most productive.

The map for Raymond Becker from chapter 2 would be quite different from Carol's, as shown in figure 8-4. Raised in a family with very high achievement expectations, Raymond developed role models early on who were successful business professionals. The high-profile CEO or rainmaking partner in a financial services firm

FIGURE 8-3

Carol's map

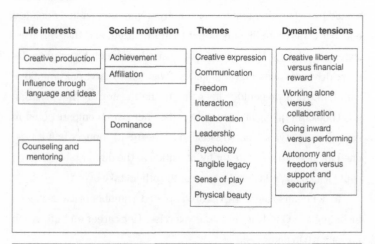

embody his internal image of success. The tasks that for him have the most meaning are those that come with the highest levels of authority within dynamic business organizations. He has often made job choices on the basis of opportunity for power and influence, at the expense of a careful examination of organizational culture or the personalities of future bosses and coworkers (sometimes with painful results). Being the boss and having influence are not only the most meaningful indications of success for Raymond, but the activities associated with these interests are also genuinely the most exciting things he can imagine doing. His strong interests in music and cinema reflect his third life interest personal high: Creative Production.

Drawing up your own map of your career and life vision can help you understand the patterns of your own life. (See "Deep Dive: The Interest and Motivation Map.")

FIGURE 8-4

Raymond's map

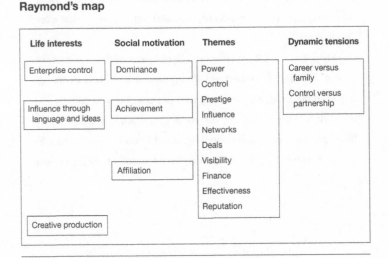

DEEP DIVE

The Interest and Motivation Map

Take some time to reflect on both your deeply embedded life interests and your social motivators. Arrange your two or three "personal high" basic interests spatially as we have done for Samantha, Carol, and Raymond. Use the distance between items on your list to indicate their relative importance.

When you have finished your life interest map, go through the same process for the three social motivators: dominance, achievement, and affiliation. If you feel your social motivators have shifted over time, diagram them for both the present time and an earlier time when you feel that they were different. Ask yourself what caused the shift.

Review the major themes and the dynamic tensions that emerged from your work with the One Hundred Jobs exercise and add them to the map. If you participated in the Image Gathering exercise, you may add themes and tensions from that exercise as well.

Stepping back from your completed map, reflect on each element. The deeply embedded life interests are unlikely to change a great deal, though at different times in your life you will express them differently. What are the most important opportunities for the expression of your personal highs right now? Are there insufficient channels for expression of one or more of your personal highs? How long has this been the case? Recall a time when you had a greater opportunity for expressing that life interest. What has changed since then?

In assessing your current life, what decisions could you make that would bring greater opportunity for the expression of this interest? What trade-offs are you willing to make to create such an opportunity?

Try to identify the most important ways to express your social motivators. What are your most important affiliative connections (both individual and group)? In what arenas can you express your power? Looking over the past year, what has made you feel you have made an important contribution? One year from now, what accomplishment will make you feel that you have achieved something personally important? Do you feel that your diagram would have been the same five or ten years ago? Do your current work and life settings provide a good context for these motivators? If not, can you imagine settings that would?

Review your list of themes. Have you missed any? Are some more important than others? Which are you realizing most fully in your life right now? Which are important but have been stifled lately? Focus on each dynamic tension individually. Spend time at each pole of the tension, allowing images, feelings, and ideas associated with that pole to surface. Now switch to the opposing pole and do the same. Do not try to "solve" the tension. Just experience it. Ultimately, you must live the resolution, not think your way through it.

Patterns in the Sand

Each of us has a self that is a rich and unique tapestry. Each of us has a pattern of personality, the carpet of a meaningful life, made of different interests and motivations. Some of us prefer to surround ourselves with other Achievers, others prefer the company of connectors. Some of us prefer more structure in our work environment and some less. Some are motivated by power, others by achievement or by relationships. Recurring interests, themes, social needs, and tensions form the signature of what is most vital for us. From this pattern we can discern the roles, relationships, and real-life environments that hold, for us, the most meaning.

We have been defining the deeper patterns of the self. Once we recognize these patterns, we will have more confidence in pursuing what we need and want, and avoiding what we do not want, amidst changing life circumstances. It is important, however, to realize that the keenest insight into these patterns, even the most sophisticated theory of personality, is itself an ephemeral image.

Tibetan Buddhism has a tradition of creating elaborate sand mandalas. These exquisitely detailed and brightly colorful depictions of deities and cosmic forces are each, in fact, elaborate models of human psychology seen from varying perspectives. Monks will take many days or even weeks to construct these large sand paintings, carefully pouring lines of the different colored sands to create the finished work of art.

Why sand? Because the last act in this meditative artistry is to sweep the sand away into a heap of mixed colors and allow this accomplished map of the human mind to return to the earth and wind. The message: all maps are constructs; all ideas of pattern are ideas. We should not confuse knowledge, no matter how subtle, with life. We must always step into life, into what is next for us, right here and now.

That is what the next part of the process is about: making a decision that allows us to act and make a meaningful change in our lives.

PART III

Getting Unstuck

Recognizing the deeper patterns of the self is not enough. We must find the will to act, even if in very small ways, so that our new imagination becomes more and more what we live every day. The final step in the cycle of impasse is integrating what we've learned so we can make a decision and take action.

NINE

Moving from
Impasse to Action

IRAWAN SUMANTRI was twenty-seven when he first came to see me. As he spoke, his friendly smile traded places with focused seriousness. He had grown up in rural Indonesia, his father an American-trained physician. He spoke admiringly of his father's altruistic decision to pass up a lucrative medical career in America and return to his rural Indonesian village to become the only Western-trained physician in the area. Dr. Sumantri was a respected leader in the region, but Irawan grew up in humble circumstances in his ancestral village. Irawan's voice dropped and his expression intensified as he talked about the poverty of the region and the violence he observed firsthand during a period of civil strife. He grew up in a world animated both by the rhythms of rural village life and by the expectations that he would attain a Western education and make a contribution as a citizen of the world.

Irawan attended college in the United States, obtaining a degree in architecture. For two years he worked as an architect for a major developer of suburban residential neighborhoods. He savored the work and went on to get his master's degree in urban planning at New York University. He married, and his first child was born a year later. After landing a position in an architectural firm, Irawan felt something was missing. His father's example loomed before him. Answering the call to work in a more altruistic organization, he joined a large economic development bank headquartered in Hong Kong. He enjoyed the work but found the organization overly bureaucratic. His compensation was also significantly less than what he could be making in the private sector. Now, as he spoke with me, he was at business school, and at an impasse. It seemed that he had done so much in his brief life, and had done so in many places. Where was his home, and what was his calling? As Irawan contemplated his next career and life move, the vision map shown in figure 9-1 emerged.

FIGURE 9-1

Irawan's map

Life interests	Social motivation	Themes	Dynamic tensions
Creative production	Achievement	Creativity Altruism Indonesia Influence Deals Learning	Creativity versus altruism Work location versus family needs
Managing people and relationships	Affiliation Dominance		

Authentic Choices

Our work at impasse leads to a moment of choice. Without action, vision can degrade into a fantasy. We must make a deliberate decision that signals a commitment, to ourselves as much as to others, that something has changed. We take out the credit card and order the lumber for the new project; we put a down payment on the house; we write the letter of resignation. But before every action there comes a final stage in the development of vision: choice. The word itself presupposes that two or more genuine and potentially meaningful alternatives have emerged. If these alternatives really represent a break into new territory, they must be based on all of the work described in the preceding chapters of this book. Authentic choices are not items we choose at our leisure from a menu somebody else hands us. They have emerged of their own accord from the images, themes, and dynamic tensions generated by the hard work at impasse. Once they have emerged, however, a tension remains; real choices, unlike convenient options, are always in tension.

In Irawan's case, it became clear that three major themes formed the core of his vision, and his impasse. Part of Irawan's difficulty was that he would often confuse these themes; a big part of the counseling effort was to help him sort them out so that he could focus on, imagine, and work through each one individually. The first theme was creativity; Creative Production was clearly Irawan's most important, deeply embedded life interest. He had a secondary area of interest in Managing People and Relationships, but this interest area was not nearly as high as Creative Production. He loved his time in architecture school and felt that his work at the drawing board was what brought him most quickly into his creative flow. He had found an outlet for this creativity with his residential design work.

The second theme was altruism, inspired by his father. This theme surfaced in the voice that whispered to him as he sat at that drafting table: "How can this help people who are truly in need? Are you directing your talents toward them? Is this the best way?"

The third theme was specific to Indonesia; Irawan felt that he, too, must ultimately contribute to his country. There were many places on the globe where his talent could help him make a contribution. Indeed, at the economic development bank, he had worked on numerous projects that had the potential to truly make a difference. None, however, offered a call as strong as his homeland. After we had identified Irawan's three central themes, we worked on the difficult choice he faced. Each theme seemed to lead to a different choice if it were given precedence. How could he choose?

Exploring the Poles

The first step in working with a dynamic tension is to go to each pole of the tension and simply focus there intently. With no agenda for making a judgment, we need to focus with free attention and note the images that emerge. Our first instinct is to flee from the uncomfortable tension, so giving ourselves over completely to just one pole is difficult. (See "Deep Dive: Riding the Tension.")

When Irawan spent time at the creativity pole, images for good work came quickly. He could see himself returning to the residential design company and becoming a lead architect for new projects. He could see himself becoming involved in the growing real estate market in Hong Kong and greater China. These images brought excitement. When focusing on the altruism pole, his images came mostly from his experience at the economic development bank.

Irawan had been a star there and knew how to make things happen in that organization. He also knew that, despite its bureaucracy, the bank was very effective and chose and executed projects well. It was the best possible platform he could imagine for effective development work.

It was more difficult to explore the Indonesia pole. His village region was economically disadvantaged and subject to sporadic civil strife. He could imagine few opportunities to put his MBA to use. Try as he might, he struggled to see any way that he could "get traction" in his home area and support his family while making a significant contribution. The voice that called him back, however, did not diminish.

The temptation when experiencing the tensions of a difficult choice is to seek a quick compromise, to find some middle ground that seems to offer some of the best of the conflicting poles. This rarely works and rarely satisfies. In the end it has the feel of something cobbled together and fleeting rather than something that asserts itself from the depths of the heart.

Irawan spent the summer between his two years at business school in Indonesia, looking at possibilities in real estate development. He was mostly disappointed—the few opportunities he could find had little to do with community development. If he wanted to build a career as an influential developer, he could do so much more rapidly elsewhere. On the community development side, he could not find any projects that could leverage his skills nearly as efficiently as his work at the economic development bank had. His attempt at compromise seemed more like the worst of both worlds than the best. Furthermore, his assessment was that there was little available in the country generally that would offer a true challenge and chance for a significant contribution.

DEEP DIVE

Riding the Tension

As you read this section, bring to mind a difficult decision you face. Allow yourself to become aware of two or three competing alternatives. Each of your alternatives will seem less than fully satisfying, as each will mean forgoing an alternative opportunity. Every decision entails loss.

Practicing free attention, spend some time at each of the poles of the decision tension in turn. Focus on that alternative and become aware of the images, associations, and feelings that come to you as you consider selecting that option. Be aware of what you will give up by doing so. Now imagine that you have made your

But Irawan's internship experience in Indonesia was a summer well spent. He got to walk the streets of the villages and the central city and talk to local community developers. Being there, and doing his thinking amidst all the feelings stirred up by his return home, paying attention to his intuition, was the only way that he could learn what he needed to move forward. He needed to make his choice with his full self rather than merely in his head. Finally, he made his decision: He would return to Indonesia to live someday, but now was not the time.

It is often helpful to take preliminary "as if" action steps before making a final choice. We all so frequently allow dynamic tensions to become abstractions that reside only in our heads, bouncing off old preconceived notions; instead we should let our full selves experience the reality of the options. We should all, when locked into decision and will go in that direction. What enters your imagination? What will the consequences be? Let yourself feel the emotional uneasiness that inevitably will arise; let yourself experience "buyer's remorse" or "decider's remorse" fully. Do not try to rationalize or justify it. Simply feel it.

You may want to jot down a few words or phrases to remind you of your experience at that pole. Stay with those images and feelings only for a few minutes, and then move on to the pole of the next alternative. With your free attention, watch what happens when you make the decision to go with the alternative that pole offers. Repeat the process for each alternative and allow yourself to experience intuitively, analytically, and emotionally what it would be like to make the decision for each.

the discomfort of the dynamic tension beneath an important choice, take action at each of the poles.

We need to talk with people who are actually working in a job located at that pole. We need to set up an informational interview or company visit so we can walk those halls and pay attention to how we feel.

The process of working with the poles of the dynamic tension is the same if we are facing a broader life decision and not a career decision. We must spend time at each of the poles and observe the feelings, thoughts, and images that come to us while we focus with our free attention. We must see what happens when we make an "as if" decision that favors whether we move to a new city or not, embark on one new project rather than another, or whatever it might be.[1] Once we have done the work of amplifying our true reactions to

DEEP DIVE

Working with the Poles of Decision

Continue to work with the same dilemma that you chose for the previous Deep Dive. Go to the pole of each alternative. For each pole, answer the following questions: With whom must you speak in order to get a better sense of what choosing this direction would mean? Is there some information that you are missing about this pole? Is there a particular place that is associated with choosing this alternative?

Next, try to take a step that will actualize your answer to each of the questions. Have a conversation with each person who came to mind while answering the first question. Read the book or do the Internet search that will give you the information that you need.

each pole, we need to test a preliminary decision by getting new information. We need to spend a month in the city we might move to or gather information about the project we are considering as if we have committed to it. We must get the decision out of our head. We need to jump in the pool and get wet. The only way forward is to bring our whole person into the tension of the choice. (See "Deep Dive: Working with the Poles of Decision.")

Giving in to Gravity

Irawan returned his focus to each of the three poles in his dynamic tension, taking with him the experiences from his summer looking into both real estate and community development possibilities in Indonesia. After he had spent time at each of the three poles of creativity, altruism, and Indonesia and we had discussed the images that had come to him, I encouraged him to sense the "heft" of each pole. All were important, but which seemed to be even heavier, more solid, and closer to his "core of meaning"?

Irawan needed to find a "base" from among these three. That is, he needed to find a way to realize one of his three themes in a deeply satisfying way, even though other aspects of that work situation might not be ideal, and even though other themes may have been restricted. A base should also hold the promise of integrating a second theme in a significant way, even if it required a significant investment of time and career building.

It was not easy work, but Irawan began to locate his center of gravity in the altruism theme. He was his father's son. He needed to feel that his work was directly affecting social well being. He began to see that he had had the strongest experience of realizing any one of his themes, in this case altruism, at the economic development bank. He wanted to be at an organization where he could put his MBA talents to full use while directly addressing social issues.

The lower level positions he had held at the bank had not offered him enough creativity, but Irawan knew that his status as a rising star would bring him greater authority and the opportunity for creativity. His plan would be to work on projects that would position him so he eventually could bring his development work to Indonesia. This sequence—choosing a base with one of the poles (in Irawan's case, altruism), with realistic promise of adding a second theme with time (for Irawan, this would be more creativity)—seemed to be the choice that made sense for him and for his family. Indonesia was impractical for now, but the bank worked in that area of Asia, and the opportunity for an eventual project in his home country was a distinct possibility. He moved his family to Hong Kong and committed to development work.

The poles in a dynamic tension do not lose their charge right away, even with a firm decision. The energy of the themes of creativity, altruism, and Indonesia will continue to resonate in Irawan's life, and he may in the future choose to give the creativity or Indonesia themes more dominance. In his work with this dynamic tension, Irawan focused on the sources of meaning at play in his personal world and gained a better understanding of what these forces are and what they ask of him. The charge that runs between two poles of a dynamic tension is an important source of life energy. The work at impasse collects that energy, but we must choose and then act, first on a trial basis and then with full commitment, in order to tap into that energy. In the end, the dynamic tension at a time of choice fuels our leap into life.

TEN

Living at the Border

LIFE AT THE BORDER is always changing. Tom Wilson was at impasse when he needed to respond to a shifting economic climate in his work as a social worker. He realized he needed to call more on the energy of the "warrior" archetype. Ten years after that impasse, his business had grown to the point where there were several people working for him. His models for efficient employee assistance programs had become popular, he was in demand as a speaker, and he traveled widely. He became an adjunct professor at a local school of social work, where he taught a popular class. He felt energized by his demanding schedule and the opportunities that presented themselves. In looking back over those ten years, he was amazed at how the rhythm of his life had changed.

He was now an entrepreneur as much as he was a social worker. He was reaching a much larger audience with his teaching and speaking than he had as a therapist. Friends and colleagues would commonly remark, "How do you do it all?"

There was another story, however. Tom was spending much less time as counselor, and he missed this. He was still a counselor at heart and felt that in working with clients he could make his biggest, even if less visible and less financially profitable, contribution. He was often away from home, sometimes for two weeks at a time. He had less time for reading. In the back of his mind, he worried that his life had become too "horizontal"—constantly moving forward—and less "vertical"—allowing him to go deep with meditation, reading, being with his family, or taking long walks in the country. He began to fit more meditation retreats into his busy schedule.

The work we do at impasse enhances our flexibility and allows us to become more comfortable "living at the border," where uncertainty, ambiguity, and dynamic tension reign. We learn that we are more alive when we live at the edge, and we come to relish the prospect of "frontier living." Each impasse brings us another taste of what such a life might be. Eventually, we become convinced that the border is where we want to be.

The night after one of his meditation retreats, Tom Wilson had a dream:

A traveler at a train station in a remote part of East Africa is in a hurry to catch the next train because he has important business. He is stuck, however, in the ticket line. The ticket seller, dressed in somewhat shabby clothes, is a dignified middle-aged African man. His posture is straight, and his easy, slow gestures are elegant. He is taking his time because he has immense patience and fully accepts his humble position as a ticket agent at a remote train station, is. He has nowhere to hurry to because he is fully at home. His calmness provides a striking counterpoint to the urgent insistence of the traveler. The traveler begins to gesture and lean forward, as if to say, "Let's get this line moving, I need to be somewhere else." The ticket seller is not perturbed; he continues to radiate acceptance and deep calm.

Tom allowed the images of the dream to work on him. He knew well the anxious insistence of that traveler; he could feel it in his body. He felt somewhat ashamed to identify with the anxious, impatient Western businessman pushing his way through the world, alienating those around him with his relentless pursuit of his own agenda. Tom, who had traveled in Africa the year before, also knew the calm dignity of the ticket seller. He knew this figure in his body as well; he had just come from many days of sitting in meditation.

In turning the dream over and experiencing the images as deeply as possible, Tom realized that a shift was taking place. His relation with the warrior part of himself had been fruitful, but the dream insisted that he pay attention to another archetypal figure—the African ticket seller who hovered at his border. Tom recognized that there is no such thing as a single, neat "shadow figure" that, once recognized and acknowledged, brings an enduring state of psychological balance; many aspects of the self need integration. In dream or folklore, a beggar or humble stranger may represent the calm that comes with seeing and accepting things as they really are. This figure does not displace the warrior, but rather offers the possibility for developing a different type of power. Tom sensed that, as he approached his midfifties, it would be the wise African man, not the warrior, who would offer the best counsel.

New Territory

"How can I tell when I am at an impasse?" I am often asked. At other times, people tell me a story about being stuck and say, "Yes, that happened to me once." In their attempts to locate impasse at a particular moment, these people miss an important point. When we describe impasse, we tell a story about when we "hit the wall" and what we had to do to get beyond it. Each story, including the stories in this book, seems to have a beginning, a middle, and an end. But this is mostly an illusion.

An impasse experience can unfold over a year or within twenty-four hours. Impasse is a psychological process, outside of time and space. It is another word for a border that is always there, beckoning. Our work at impasse helps us cross that border and live in a new territory. In this sense, impasse is the frontier of what needs to happen next for us if we are to live life as openly as possible. If we lived completely openly, we would probably not experience impasse, because we would face each moment without any evasions, excuses, or attachments to old habits.

Few of us are capable of living continually in such a fashion, however, so we experience "impasse crises" like the ones described in this book. An impasse crisis happens when we have been, for some time, avoiding the work of living fully at our border. We are missing something essential in our lives, and it is as if the impasse crisis is saying, "Enough! No more evasion! You can no longer avoid this, you must deal with it now or these symptoms will persist and grow more intense." If we could live all of the time at the border, there would be no need for this message.

Living at the Border

What would it be like to *live* at the border? What would it be like to be open fully to the energies and possibilities that are emerging, regardless of their threat to habit, comfort, and stereotyped expectations? The lives of artists give us a glimpse of the answer to this question. In one sense, their very work is to make their experience at impasse visible, or audible, to others. Their lives often become metaphors for what experience at the edge of impasse would be like.

Martin Scorsese's film *No Direction Home* focuses on just five years in the life of Bob Dylan, 1961 to 1966. For Dylan, these were years of volcanic creativity. Song after startling song emerged as he changed musical genres and produced music of astounding variety and compelling originality. His growing audience grew confused, and even angry, at his shifting identity. But no amount of audience hostility, media criticism, or fatigue from concerts stops him. He is in the flow. This is the image of a person living continually at the edge, with no fear of the consequences.

Similarly, D. H. Lawrence lived a life of intense devotion to beauty, art, and the world of relationship throughout his thirties and early forties (he died at forty-four). He believed that a person's greatest art was his life and held that the manner in which he crafted his life was far more important than the craft, or outcome, of his writing. Lawrence had some public recognition in his last years, but for the most part he devoted those years to what he called a "savage pilgrimage" in search of beauty in a "sense of place" and of deeper companionship with the men and women around him. His love of song, the earth, and the sensual world was his great "accomplishment." He seemed to live continually at the border.

Although they are able to tell us about it, life at the border is not reserved for artists. It is, for each of us, the only way forward.

All of the world religions offer some variation on Lawrence's notion of life as pilgrimage. In Judaism, the exodus from the captivity of the spirit to new life is a central theme. In Christianity, the Gospel tells us that the Son of Man "has no place to rest His head." In Islam, the hajj is a constant pilgrimage toward the Divine, as much as it is a journey to Mecca. The message of the major faiths is not, at its heart, a measure of dogmatic certainties, but of a journey forward that breaks through times of trial along the way.

This book has concerned itself with the way we might begin the journey anew when we accept the way we are stuck and do the work of disciplined observation and imagination. The experience at impasse is both tough and exciting. It is like a cold autumn wind that carries the thrill of color and change. Impasse invites us to shed our fears and move to the border of what is actually presenting itself to us, right now. This returning offers us a bargain, an opportunity to exchange certainty for vulnerability, sentimentality for depth of feeling, and the comfort of the familiar for the energy of a world that, as hard and exciting as it may be, is always beckoning.

Continuing the Journey

An Annotated Bibliography

T HE IDEAS elaborated in this book, even the findings of my original research, are in many ways inseparable from the ideas of the psychologists, sociologists, philosophers, psychotherapists, and poets upon which they rest. However, I chose to write this book without the encumbrance of footnotes to bring you directly into the experience of the work at impasse. Thus the book is not a treatise on the ideas that support the work, and its tone is deliberately one of immediacy rather than abstraction. Those ideas do provide the deeper, and richer, underpinnings of the work. Therefore, I share my sources with you here, so that you can pursue in greater depth those ideas that you find most compelling, meaningful, and useful.

Readings for the Introduction

"The psychologist Mihaly Csikszentmihalyi would say that at times such as these we are 'in the flow' . . ."

In a now-classic study, Mihaly Csikszentmihalyi, a psychologist at the University of Chicago, studied the experience of being deeply engaged and satisfied while working. To do so, he had workers from many different walks of life, at the sound of a buzzer, make note of what they were doing and how they were feeling at that moment of working. Csikszentmihalyi found that work, regardless of the type, when most satisfying and engaging was accompanied by a sense of being "in a flow," which he described as "the state in which people are so involved in an activity that nothing else seems to matter; the experience itself is so enjoyable that people will do it even at great cost, for the sheer sake of doing it . . ." You can read about the practical application of Mihaly Csikszentmihalyi's research in *Flow: The Psychology of Optimal Experience* (New York: Harper Perennial, 1991), 4.

Readings for Chapter 1: Facing Crisis

"In recent decades, developmental psychologists have created highly useful theoretical models . . ."

Noteworthy are Erik Erikson, Daniel Levinson, Carol Gilligan, Lawrence Kohlberg, Robert Kegan, and William Perry. Each is an important theorist whose model of human development describes a process of maturation that requires moving beyond the issues and models of earlier stages of development. Each, in his or her own way, talks about the role of a crisis or the failure of a mental model in precipitating a movement to a more mature level of development. Erik Erikson's classic work is *Childhood and Society* (New York: Norton, 1950), in which he presents the eight-stage developmental theory that became, during the second half of the twentieth century, the touchstone for many developmental theorists. His book breaks ground in the psychoanalytic tradition by moving its focus beyond the first five years of life, which so captivated Freud and his immediate followers, to include the full human life cycle. Erikson is a good writer, and both the book and his ideas are readily accessible.

Daniel Levinson in his well-known *The Seasons of a Man's Life* (New York: Knopf, 1978) provides the first contemporary longitudinal study of a group of men as they transition through the midlife period of ages thirty-five to fifty. His intent, through his research process of extensive interviewing, was "to create a theory of adult development, from the entry into adulthood until the late forties." The strength of the book is in the rigor of Levinson's interviewing and analysis. Its weakness is clear in its title—it is a book about men exclusively. The focus on male psychology found in the majority of early- and mid-twentieth-century studies, and generalizations about the nature of human development extrapolated from the research and personal experience of mostly male psychologists, was a weakness sorely in need of correction by the latter half of the century.

Notable among those who rose to this challenge is Carol Gilligan, whose best-known book is *In a Different Voice: Psychological Theory and Women's Development* (Cambridge, MA: Harvard University Press, 1982). In this book, Gilligan challenges the strong focus of developmental psychologists on separation from parental ties and individuation through individual achievement as being the most important hallmarks of healthy development. In a prose style that is simultaneously rigorous and elegant, she makes the point that a vital dimension of the human experience is missing from such models: the capacity for relationship.

Gilligan found that a capacity for relationship was central to the way in which the women in her study made choices and developed values. She questions how there can be true maturity without a deepening capacity for intimate relationship, and she contends that the female developmental experience has a different emphasis from the male experience, a *relational* emphasis. Her work points directly to the way in which this experience has been undervalued not only in the thinking of developmental psychologists, but in the broader culture generally. Other important writers on the importance of gender differences in developmental psychology include Karen Horney, Nancy Chodorow, and Julia Kristeva.

Jean Piaget, whose seminal work (written with B. Inhelder) is *The Growth of Logical Thinking from Childhood to Adolescence* (New York: Basic Books, 1958), inspired the work of, among countless others, two major thinkers in developmental psychology in the 1970s and 1980s: Lawrence Kohlberg and Robert Kegan. Kohlberg (*The Philosophy of Moral Development*, San Francisco: Harper & Row, 1981) studied moral development and identified stages of progressively more mature moral reasoning. (Carol Gilligan critiqued his emphasis on "justice" as the primary context of moral concern to the exclusion of "care" as the springboard for her highly influential delineation of the relational dimension of development, cited above.)

Kegan (*The Evolving Self: Problem and Process in Human Development*, Cambridge, MA: Harvard University Press, 1982) uses Piaget's theory of the structure of cognitive development as a model for looking at the way in which self-identity develops. For Kegan, each new iteration of the self emerges when incongruities between our understanding of the world and new experience point to the inadequacy of our current mental model and demand a larger and more inclusive apprehension of our own "self." Kegan's approach is useful in understanding what is happening when we do the work with dynamic tensions discussed in chapter 3. William Perry (*Forms of Intellectual and Ethical Development in the College Years*, New York: Holt, Rinehart and Winston 1968) also focused on stages of self-development, but with a particular focus on the college-age developmental era.

"Myths illuminate subtle aspects of the human condition and human development . . ."

Through the centuries, cultures have relied on myths to pass on their accumulated wisdom concerning developmental psychology. The best introduction to this perspective on comparative mythology remains Joseph Campbell's classic, *The Hero with a Thousand Faces* (Princeton, NJ: Princeton University Press, 1968).

"This information is what philosopher and psychologist Eugene Gendlin calls the implicit . . ."

You can read about Eugene Gendlin's philosophy of the implicit in *Experiencing and the Creation of Meaning* (Evanston, IL: Northwestern University Press, 1996) but most people become familiar with his highly practical approach to self-understanding through his book *Focusing* (New York: Bantam, 1982). Gendlin is concerned with the way we know the totality of our immediate situation before we represent that knowing to ourselves as language. In translation into language, a lot of the complexity, especially the emotional complexity, of the situation is lost. Our "head brain," as Gendlin would say, sees things in simplistic, black-and-white ways. It creates a convenient code of our reality so that we can be more efficient. This efficiency, however, ends up leaving a lot of our experience, and our meaning, behind. Our "body brain," however, retains the fullness of the experience and all of the echoes from our personal emotional history that it carries.

Focusing is a practical, step-by-step, way to establish a dialog between the "head brain" and the "body brain" and recover a fuller sense of the meaning of a situation. The book *Focusing* is probably the best place to begin if you want to further explore this particular way of "going to your boundary." Another useful guide to the focusing process is Ann Weiser Cornell's *The Radical Acceptance of Everything* (Berkeley, CA: Calluna Press, 2005). You can facilitate the focusing process by working with a focusing partner. For more about certified teachers of focusing, you can contact the Focusing Institute in Spring Valley, New York.

> "When we find ourselves at impasse, we all begin to tell a story that explains our sense of being stuck or lost . . ."

For several decades, psychologists have been exploring the way in which we construct our world by constructing personal narratives or stories, or by accepting, without analysis, the stories others tell about us. The very fact that someone comes to a counselor's office is in itself a statement that those stories are losing their usfulness. The person coming for help, however, may or may not acknowledge this. She comes into the room bringing her best description of why she is there and what is going on, along with her best assessment of what her options may be. This story that she brings to a counselor represents her current mental model of the difficulty she is encountering and how she might respond, of who she is, and, in the background, of how the world generally works. If this were a big enough story, a good enough story, a story that embraced all of the paradoxes and uncertainties she faces, she would have no need to visit a counselor.

Michael White and David Epston (*Narrative Means to Therapeutic Ends*, New York: Norton, 1990) are leaders in applying to the counseling process the ways in which people develop a sense of self through the construction of personal narratives. They extend to the counseling realm the work of psychologists such as Jerome Bruner (*Acts of Meaning*, Cambridge, MA: Harvard University Press, 1990) and Kenneth Gergen (*An Invitation to Social Construction*, Thousand Oaks, CA: Sage Publications, 2000), and philosophers such as Gregory Bateson (*Mind and Nature: A Necessary Unity*, New York: Dutton, 1979) and Michael Foucault (*Power/Knowledge: Selected Interviews and Other Writings*, New York: Pantheon, 1980). All of these thinkers have focused on the importance of narrative in understanding the reality of an individual person.

Readings for Chapter 3: Opening Up and Letting Go

"The problem with any mental model is that it is always operating on information from the past . . ."

Philosophers have described with great subtlety the way in which we create mental models that must be abandoned for deeper thinking or more direct ways of knowing. Plotinus (*The Enneads*, Stephen McKenna, trans., Burdett, NY: Larson Publications, 1992) is an example from the ancient world; Martin Heidegger (*Basic Writings*, New York: Harper & Row, 1977), Alfred Korzybski (*Science and Sanity: An Introduction to Non-Aristotelian Systems and General Semantics*, Englewood, NJ: Institute of General Semantics, 1995), and R. A. Schwaller de Lubicz (*Nature Word:*

Verbe Nature, Great Barrington, MA: Lindisfarne Books, 1982), are contemporary examples. Peter Berger and Thomas Luckman (*The Social Construction of Reality: A Treatise on the Social Construction of Reality*, Garden City, NY: Anchor Books, 1967) look at the construction of mental models from a sociological perspective.

"A first step is to practice 'free attention' . . ."

The practice of free attention lies at the heart of the meditation practices of both the Zen and Insight Meditation (Vipassana) traditions. There are many excellent books available about these traditions. Bernard Glassman and Rick Fields provide a solid introduction to the Zen approach in *Instructions to the Cook: A Zen Master's Lessons on Living a Life That Matters* (New York: Harmony Books, 1996). Glassman is one of the most respected contemporary teachers of Zen. Robert Kennedy's *Zen Gifts to Christians* (London: Continuum, 2000) is also excellent. For a basic introduction to the practice of Insight Meditation, Larry Rosenberg's *Breath by Breath: The Liberating Practice of Insight Meditation* (Boston: Shambhala Publications, 2004) and Joseph Goldstein's *Insight Meditation: The Practice of Freedom* (Boston: Shambhala Publications, 2003) are good places to start.

From the Image Gathering exercise available at www.careerleader.com/gettingunstuck

". . . elements I have taken from my work with Jungian analysts, from various meditation teachers, from the work of Dr. Milton Erikson . . ."

I provide sources for meditation practice above, and refer to my Jungian teachers below. Milton Erikson, widely known for his work with therapeutic hypnosis, was a genius who could help his patients shift the experience of their lives to less encumbering "stories" and broader contexts. His works can be difficult to locate but his ideas are accessible through the books of his students, such as Sidney Rosen, *My Voice Will Go With You: The Teaching Tales of Milton H. Erickson, M.D.* (W.W. Norton, New York, 1991) and Jay Haley, *Uncommon Therapy: The Psychiatric Techniques of Milton H. Erickson, M.D.* (W.W. Norton, New York, 1993).

Readings for Chapter 4:
Shifting to a New Understanding

"We must learn how to let the images work on us before we can begin the work of appreciating the coded messages they bear . . ."

The work with images portrayed in chapter 4 comes from my many years as a student of Jungian and archetypal psychology. Archetypal psychology studies the images that represent the essence of both culture and the individual human experience within that culture. This outgrowth of the Jungian perspective looks to understand trends in contemporary culture, as well as the psychological difficulties individuals experience, and the way those trends and difficulties are represented in images found in architecture, popular art, political discourse, legal documents, fashion, or the dreams of a client in psychotherapy.

A primary dictum of archetypal psychology, provided by American psychologist James Hillman, is "follow the image." In other words, do not overlay the image with theory or analysis based on models derived from previous experience. The image is a messenger for a larger paradigm than the one you have in mind. This is true if you are standing in front of a statue in the Louvre, as we did with Rilke in chapter 4, trying to wrestle with feelings of anxiety or depression, or reading Shakespeare (or Einstein, for that matter).

Hillman is the leading figure in contemporary archetypal psychology. A good introduction to his work is the anthology edited by Thomas Moore, *A Blue Fire: Selected Writings by James Hillman* (New York: Harper & Row, 1989). Other important books by Hillman include *The Dream and the Underworld* (New York: Harper & Row, 1979) and *Re-visioning Psychology* (New York: Harper & Row, 1975). Thomas Moore himself is an important author in this field. His books take the ideas and approach of archetypal psychology into the territory of everyday life and include *Care of the Soul* (New York: HarperCollins, 1992) and *Dark Nights of the Soul* (New York: Gotham Books, 2004). Other important authors in the tradition of archetypal psychology include Raphael Lopez-Pedraza, Murray Stein, Adolf Guggenbuhl-Craig, David Miller, Henri Corbin, and Robert Sardello. A very good book on letting your dreams "work on you" is Robert Bosnak's *A Little Course in Dreams* (Boston: Shambhala Publications, 1988).

Readings for Chapter 5:
Our Deepest Interests:
The First Pattern in the Carpet

"Insight into the pattern of our deeply embedded life interests allows us to better predict the activities, work environments, living circumstances, and types of people that we will find most fulfilling . . ."

Much of my academic training in psychology has been in the scientific empiricist tradition, particularly as it applies to personality structure and to the process and outcomes of counseling and psychotherapy. Large-scale empirical studies of human interest patterns, pioneered by psychologists such as E. K. Strong (*Vocational Interests of Men and Women*, Stanford, CA: Stanford University Press, 1943) have been important in identifying the relationship between personality structure and meaningful work. The most influential contemporary theorist of work interests is John Holland (*Making Vocational Choices: A Theory of Vocational Personalities and Work Environments*, 3rd ed., Odessa, FL: Psychological Assessment Resources, 1997) who identified six fundamental themes underlying human work interests. His model has been rigorously researched and validated for more than forty years.

In my own research with James Waldroop, I focused on the basic elements of human interest as they are expressed in business work. You can read more about the application of this research in *Discovering Your Career in Business* (New York: Basic Books, 1997). For a more technical and detailed exposition of our theory and assessment methods, see "A Function Centered Model of Interest Assessment for Business Careers" (*Journal of Career Assessment*, 12, no. 3, August 2004). In "Job Sculpting: The Art of Retaining Your Best People" (*Harvard Business Review*, September–October 1999) we presented a model for managers to use in helping their employees craft work roles that would be more meaningful and inspiring. Career Leader, the psychological self-assessment program that developed out of this research, is available at www.careerleader.com.

Readings for Chapter 6:
Learning to Let Our Passions Guide Us

"In my conversations with students and clients, inevitably the question of talent emerges. "I now know what I want," my client says "but can I really do it or is it just a fantasy? . . ."

In addition to my observation that, over long periods of time, skills follow interests, it is also important to recognize that psychological research over the past several decades has shown that a very big part of the answer to the question "Can I do it?" is "Do you truly *believe* that you can do it?" Many factors affect the willingness and ability to perform well, but the most important factor according to psychologist Albert Bandura is *self-efficacy*. Self-efficacy is one of the most respected, durable, and tested theories of human performance to emerge in the latter half of the twentieth century. It currently exerts a very strong influence on the field of cognitive psychology. Bandura's most comprehensive report on his theory is his *Self Efficacy: The Exercise of Control* (New York: W. H. Freeman, 1997).

Readings for Chapter 7:
Power, People, and Achievement:
Three Interwoven Patterns in the Carpet

"A shorthand to expression of these three needs is: power, people, and achievement . . ."

You can read more about Henry Murray's theory of fundamental social needs in *Explorations in Personality* (New York: Wiley, 1938) and about David McClelland's in *Human Motivation* (Cambridge: Cambridge University Press, 1988) and in McClelland's *Harvard Business Review* article (with David Burnham), "Power Is the Great Motivator" (*Harvard Business Review* OnPoint Edition, February 2000).

"In *Kinds of Power*, psychologist James Hillman explored the ways in which power is evident in the human world . . ."

What Hillman does so well is enrich our imagination of concepts by evoking etymology, myth, biography, case history, and the history of ideas in order to reveal the subtlety and complexity that underlie common abstractions such as "power." The reference here is *Kinds of Power* (New York: Currency Doubleday, 1995).

Readings for Chapter 9:
Moving from Impasse to Action

From Note 1: "These are the four domains of consciousness that Carl Jung described in great detail . . ."

Much has appeared in the popular psychological press about Jung's theory of types and its widespread application. It is highly doubtful that Jung ever intended his theory to lead to a system for classifying individuals into specific types. He did assert, however, that there is an innate orientation toward one of his "judgment" functions (Thinking or Feeling) and one of his "perception" functions (Sensing or Intuition) as well as an innate orientation in the "attitude" of consciousness (Introversion or Extroversion). The best source will always be Jung himself in volume six of his *Collected Works, Psychological Types* (Princeton, NJ: Princeton University Press, 1977). The best interpreter of his theory is his colleague and fellow analyst, Marie-Louise Von Franz, *Lectures on Jung's Typology* (London: Continuum, 1971).

As Jung's *Collected Works* (Princeton, NJ: Princeton University Press) run to twenty volumes, approaching Jung can be intimidating. Many first take him up with one of his overview books such as *Memories, Dreams, Reflections* (New York: Vintage, 1989) or *The Undiscovered Self* (New York: Signet, 1959). Another excellent starting point is *The Portable Jung* (Joseph Campbell, ed., New York: Penguin, 1976), which has Campbell's very helpful introduction.

The readings given in this appendix are not exhaustive; they are entry points—highly regarded overviews that can lead you deeper into the literature of the area they cover. A good way to move forward is to follow your excitement: When you find an author who speaks to you, follow the trail to the authors who have inspired him or her. In this way, your reading follows a deeper instinct, a passion that is already there and looking for elaboration and confirmation. These books then become what they actually are, the records of fellow travelers.

A Note on Impasse and Depression

IMPASSE often brings with it an intermittent heaviness of mood. During times of impasse, it may seem that usually reliable resources for cheering yourself up or thinking your way through problems are no longer effective. In many ways, you may feel that business as usual in the way you take care of things has slowed, or even halted. You may feel that you are "not yourself" and that your familiar pleasures and distractions no longer hold their appeal. You may loose sleep turning over an important decision in your mind. In all of these ways, a career or life impasse may mimic some of the symptoms of depression. It is important to realize that these symptoms, and the impasse experience, are not, in themselves, evidence of clinical depression.

The official definition of depression, as stated in the *Diagnostic and Statistical Manual of Mental Disorders* of the American Psychiatric Association is actually a menu. It presents a list of nine symptoms, five of which must be "present during the same two-week period and represent a change from previous functioning."[1] The symptoms are as follows:

- Depressed mood, "most of the day, nearly every day"

- Notably decreased interest in usual pleasures "in all, or almost all, activities most of the day, nearly every day"

- A marked increase or decrease in appetite that, again, occurs "nearly every day"

- Difficulty sleeping or notable oversleeping, "nearly every day"

- Nearly every day feeling either unusually restless or unusually slowed-down

- Feeling unusual fatigue, every day

- Daily feelings of worthlessness or inappropriate guilt

- Notable difficulty concentrating or making decisions, every day

- Recurring thoughts of death or ideas of committing suicide

We can sum up the difference between these symptoms at impasse and during an episode of clinical depression in two words: duration and intensity. During times of impasse, some of these symptoms may appear intermittently, but they are rarely present all of the time for weeks on end. It is unusual to experience them "most of the day, every day." Their intensity is typically much less than what individuals report during episodes of clinical depression. They may be painful but they do not shut down your ability to move through your day and feel that you can meet the challenges in front of you even if you feel "in the dark."

Accepting the darker emotional tones of impasse is part of the journey. In all classic descriptions of impasse, this sense of darkness is part of the story. Whether it is Dante lost in his "dark wood," Odysseus journeying to Hades in the eleventh book of the *Odyssey*, or Holden Caulfield stuck wondering what he should do next with his life, this emotional heaviness seems to come with the territory.

At the same time, neither impasse nor depression is a time for going it alone. Help for most of us comes in the form of a good friend. There are times, however, when it is wise to reach out beyond our immediate circle. A great danger of clinical depression is its ability to place you in a rut where biochemical imbalances undermine your best efforts at moving forward, and even your initiative for seeking the help you need. Research has shown that, when clinical depression is truly present, the best treatment is a combination of medication and psychotherapy. If you are experiencing several of the symptoms listed above, and they are persisting, I encourage you to have at least an initial conversation with your physician, or some other trusted professional counselor. Your local hospital, HMO, or the counseling service of a local university, are good sources for such a referral.

Scoring the
One Hundred Jobs Exercise

I N THE COLUMN on the left, find the twelve jobs that
you found the most exciting when you participated in
the One Hundred Jobs exercise in chapter 4. Give one point to each
of the basic interest areas that appear in the column to the right of
each of your twelve choices. Add up the number of points for each
of the ten basic interest areas to determine your top two or three
"personal high" deeply embedded life interests. If you have several
ties or close scorings that indicate more than two or three personal
highs, go back to chapter 5 and read the sections relevant to each
of these interest areas and determine which two or three are truly
most important to you.

Find your top twelve job choices	**Score one point for each of these basic interest dimensions**
1. Marketing researcher	Professor
2. Child care worker	Coach
3. Computer software designer	Engineer
4. Sports coach	Coach, Action Hero, Team Leader
5. Manager at a manufacturing plant	Team Leader
6. Salesperson in a retail store	Persuader, Organizer
7. Social services professional	Coach
8. Salesperson for high-tech products	Persuader
9. Litigator	Persuader
10. Psychotherapist	Coach
11. Manager of a retail store	Team Leader
12. Public relations professional	Persuader
13. Advertising executive	Artist, Persuader
14. TV talk show host	Persuader
15. Theologian	Professor
16. Speech therapist	Coach
17. Newscaster	Persuader
18. Secretary	Organizer
19. Automobile mechanic	Action Hero
20. Electrician	Action Hero
21. Entertainer (singer, comedian, etc.)	Artist
22. Optometrist	Action hero, Professor
23. Professional actor	Artist
24. Senior hospital manager	Team Leader, Boss
25. Fine artist	Artist
26. School superintendent	Coach, Team Leader, Boss
27. Leader of a product-development team	Team Leader, Boss
28. Religious counselor	Coach
29. Financial analyst	Number Cruncher
30. TV or film director	Persuader, Artist
31. Personal financial advisor	Number Cruncher
32. Director of human resources	Team Leader, Coach
33. Graphic designer	Artist
34. Economist	Number Cruncher, Professor
35. Business strategy consultant	Professor, Boss

36.	Homemaker	Organizer
37.	Senior military leader	Boss
38.	Chief executive officer	Boss
39.	Librarian	Organizer
40.	Research and development manager	Engineer, Professor
41.	Real estate developer	Boss
42.	Music composer	Artist
43.	Veterinarian	Action Hero
44.	Advertising copywriter	Artist, Persuader
45.	Senior manager of a manufacturing business	Team Leader, Boss
46.	Nurse	Coach
47.	Ship captain	Boss, Action Hero
48.	Research sociologist	Professor
49.	Manager of information systems	Team Leader, Engineer, Number Cruncher
50.	Investigative reporter	Artist, Persuader
51.	Medical researcher	Engineer, Professor
52.	Chief financial officer	Boss, Number Cruncher
53.	Office manager	Team leader, organizer
54.	Police officer	Action Hero
55.	Investment banker	Number Cruncher, Boss
56.	Manager of a restaurant	Team Leader
57.	Entrepreneur	Boss
58.	Vacation resort manager	Team Leader
59.	Electrical engineer	Engineer
60.	High school teacher	Coach
61.	Professor of political science	Professor
62.	Theoretical physicist	Professor, Number Cruncher
63.	Computer systems analyst	Engineer
64.	Fiction writer	Artist
65.	Newspaper editor	Artist, Persuader
66.	University professor	Professor
67.	Military serviceperson	Action Hero
68.	Diplomat	Persuader
69.	Venture capitalist	Boss
70.	Military strategist	Professor
71.	Logistical planner	Engineer, Number Cruncher

72.	City planner	Artist
73.	Accountant	Organizer, Number Cruncher
74.	Bank manager	Team Leader
75.	Architect	Artist
76.	Carpenter	Action Hero
77.	Manufacturing process engineer	Engineer
78.	Firefighter	Action hero
79.	Marketing brand manager	Boss, Team Leader
80.	Surgeon	Action Hero
81.	Investment manager	Number Cruncher
82.	Stockbroker	Number Cruncher
83.	Director of nonprofit organization	Coach, Team Leader
84.	Event planner	Organizer
85.	Administrative assistant	Organizer
86.	Credit manager	Organizer, Number Cruncher
87.	Elected public official	Persuader, Boss
88.	Motivational speaker	Persuader
89.	Mayor of a city or town	Boss, Persuader
90.	President of a community charity	Boss
91.	Real estate salesperson	Persuader
92.	Professional athlete	Action Hero
93.	Clerical worker	Organizer
94.	Foreign trade negotiator	Persuader
95.	Bookkeeper	Organizer
96.	Emergency medical technician	Action Hero, Coach
97.	Statistician	Number Cruncher
98.	Manager of a stock or bond mutual fund	Number Cruncher
99.	Proofreader	Organizer
100.	Civil engineer	Action Hero, Engineer

Chapter One

1. I have changed client names and some of the details of their stories to pre-serve confidentiality.

2. In particular see the work of Erik Erikson, Daniel Levinson, Carol Gilligan, Lawrence Kohlberg, Robert Kegan, and William Perry. References are provided in the annotated bibliography.

3. Eugene Gendlin uses the term "felt sense" in *Focusing* (New York: Bantam, 1982) to describe the "hunch," or sense that presents itself physically, in our bodies, as a first inkling that something beneath our full awareness requires our attention.

Chapter Two

1. An excellent introduction to the way in which we actually recover the shadow is Robert Bly's *A Little Book on the Human Shadow* (San Francisco, Harper & Row, 1988). I have learned much from Bly's writing on both the Shadow and the Accuser.

2. You can read more about Eugene Gendlin's approach to working with the inner critic in *Focusing-Oriented Psychotherapy* (New York: Guilford Press, 1996).

3. A number of Eugene Gendlin's students in the focusing process have taken an altogether different attitude toward the Inner Critic. Notable among them is Ann Weiser Cornell who in her book, *The Radical Acceptance of Everything* (Berkeley, CA: Calluna Press, 2005), asks the question, "Who exactly is this critic if not an 'exiled' part of our very self?" She suggests that pushing the critic away will only prolong the bitterness of his exile, causing him to speak with an even louder voice when given a chance to do so. She suggests instead that we treat the Accuser like any other part of the self that is desperate to be heard and ask it: "What are you feeling that leads you to manifest this way?" Cornell suggests that there is typically one answer to this question: the Accuser is afraid.

It was attacking so fiercely because it was afraid that something would go wrong, that something wouldn't get fixed, that other people would be critical. A fear of being shamed, or not approved of, or left out often underlies the attack. Seen from this perspective, we may come to recognize the fierce Accuser as a shamed child, desperate for attention and approval, desperate to be let into the circle of full awareness and acceptance, desperate to connect.

From this point of view, the best way to respond to the Accuser is to open the door and let it into the room where it can take its place around the table and enjoy the pleasure of acceptance and the warmth of the hearth of attention. In this way, open arms, not a pushing or waving away, allows you to neutralize the Accuser toxin. Such an embrace requires the ability to take a neutral, meditative stance during the Accuser's attack. (This art of "free attention" is the subject of the next chapter.)

Wave away or embrace? There are times, perhaps, when each is appropriate. During a fierce attack, when it is hard to find free attention and when the Accuser is stopping you from taking immediate action that is growth-enhancing, the waving away may be most effective. On the other hand, there is energy in the Accuser waiting to be released; trying to listen as closely as possible to the feelings behind the attack will be a gesture that offers the possibility of insight and healing.

Chapter Three

1. The translation here is by Stephen Mitchell, from *The Selected Poetry of Rainer Maria Rilke* (New York: Vintage International, 1989).

Chapter Four

1. *The Archetypes and the Collective Unconscious*, volume 9:1, *Collected Works of C.G. Jung* (Princeton: Princeton University Press, 1959).

2. *Meno*, translated by W. K. C. Guthrie in *Plato, The Collected Dialogues* edited by Edith Hamilton and Huntington Cairns (Princeton: Princeton University Press, 1961).

Chapter Five

1. K. S. Douglas Low, Mijung Yoon, Brent W. Roberts, and James Rounds, "The Stability of Vocational Interests from Early Adolescence to Middle Adulthood: A Quantitative Review of Longitudinal Studies," *Psychological Bulletin*, volume 131:5, 2005.

2. John Holland's theory of human interests is the model accepted most widely among contemporary career psychologists. His model of career interests actually describes six major themes, two of which we use to complete the core-function model. See Holland's *Making Vocational Choices: A Theory of Vocational Personalities*

and Work Environments, 3rd ed. (Odessa, FL: Psychological Assessment Resources, 1997).

3. Holland identifies this basic interest as the "Realistic" theme.

4. Holland identifies this basic interest as the "Conventional" theme.

Chapter Six

1. Søren Kierkegaard, *The Sickness unto Death* (New York: Penguin Classics, 1989).

Chapter Seven

1. In the twentieth century, American psychologist Henry Murray pioneered the study of human personality as a constellation of fundamental social needs. He identified a wide range of these needs and developed methods for measuring which needs are most important to a given individual. See *Explorations in Personality* (New York: Wiley, 1938). Following in this tradition, psychologist David McClelland placed a particular emphasis on three of the needs Murray identified: power, affiliation, and achievement. He felt each person's profile on these three dimensions provided essential information about how that individual would participate in an organization. See *Human Motivation* (Cambridge: Cambridge University Press, 1988).

2. James Hillman, *Kinds of Power* (New York: Currency Doubleday, 1995).

Chapter Nine

1. When we make an "as if" decision and take preliminary action, we have the opportunity to bring all aspects of our consciousness to the decision: thinking, feeling, intuition, and sensing. These are the four domains of consciousness that Carl Jung described in great detail. In Jung's model, each of us is dominant in one of the four, and we "lead" with that domain when we attempt to understand the world and make decisions. (Jung provides overviews of his theories in *Memories, Dreams, Reflections*, New York: Vintage Press, 1989, and *The Undiscovered Self*, New York: Signet, 1959.) When faced with impasse, however, no single mode of awareness can capture the import of a significant life change.

Impasse forces us out of the comfort of our dominant mode; it stretches us to use more of our awareness to select the option that makes sense and feels right. The decision must come from the head, the heart, *and* the gut. Preliminary action can be helpful, since it forces us to engage the world. It shakes things up when we must set up an interview, travel to a different place, research a new topic, and talk to new people. We are bringing more of ourselves, and not just our default habits, to the decision.

Jung saw the four modes of consciousness as being two sets of polar opposites. Thinking and feeling are poles of one dimension, and intuition and sensing the poles of another. In my experience, the ultimate resolution of the dynamic tension beneath a major decision at impasse often comes from the pole *opposite* to our dominant mode. The thinker has thought to completion all possibilities at each pole of the choice, and then gets in touch with the strong feelings that she has for one pole rather than the other. The strong feeling type feels passionately about the opportunities at both poles, and then thinks through the consequences of each and realizes that choosing one pole is highly impractical. The strong sensing type gets confused focusing on the details of each possibility, and then has a flash of insight that reveals the bigger picture that points in one direction rather than the other. The strong intuitive type can imagine all of the possibilities of both options, but when he visits the location of each, his senses are grabbed by one setting and not the other. It is as if impasse were designed to expand our consciousness and get us out of our conditioned mode of awareness.

Appendix B

1. *Diagnostic and Statistical Manual of Mental Disorders DSM-IV,* 4th ed (American Psychiatric Association, Washington, D.C., 1994).

TIMOTHY BUTLER is a Senior Fellow on the faculty of the Harvard Business School, where he is the Director of Career Development Programs. He has been a psychologist, psychotherapist, and career development counselor for over twenty-five years. Dr. Butler's research has focused largely on how people find their way to meaningful work. His books have been translated into many languages, and his research has led to career self-assessment programs and career counseling models that are used by universities and corporations around the world. You can learn more about his work at www.career leader.com/gettingunstuck.